A TREASURY

OF THE

SPOKEN WORD

A TREASURY

OF THE

SPOKEN WORD

A COLLECTION OF FAMILIAR POEMS
ANNOTATED AND INTERPRETED
FOR READING ALOUD

TED COTT

INTRODUCTION
LOUIS UNTERMEYER

HERMITAGE PRESS, Inc.
NEW YORK 21, N. Y.

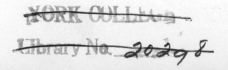

Copyright, 1949, by Ted Cott

FIRST EDITION

MANUFACTURED IN THE UNITED STATES OF AMERICA

for

Jonathan and Jeremy

"Let me count the ways . . ."

INTRODUCTION,
OR GRUDGING ADVERTISEMENT

FOR some years I have known Ted Cott as a producer (in every sense of the word), as program director, master of ceremonies, public stimulator and private friend. It is in the last capacity that I feel betrayed. When Ted as m.c. teased and twitted me on our radio program "Let's Balance the Books," I may have squirmed a few times but, after all, that was his part as well as his privilege. Anthologies, however, are something else again! As an anthologist I am, of course, aware that I have no patent on collecting and publishing assorted Treasuries, Golden Thoughts, Great Utterances, Man's Favorite Phrases and The World's Best Poems. Competition, I have been told, is the life of trade, even though it sometimes seems that every casual compatriot turns out to be a competitor. But when a friend invades what you had believed to be your particular domain, it is like an enemy poaching on your preserves, abusing your property and stabbing your royalties in the back.

Naturally, when I heard that Ted Cott was preparing an anthology, I hoped it would be a poor one. "Most anthologies," said I, with a jealous twinge, "are merely the cullings of other anthologies." All the compiler seems to need is a pair of well-sharpened shears, a pot of mucilage, and three standard collections. The requirements might even be made into a nursery rhyme:

> Scissors and paste,
> And not much taste,
> And that's what anthologies are made of.

Unfortunately for me, and fortunately for the reader, Ted Cott has not followed the expected formula. It is true that his book consists mostly of old favorites, that many of his selections are (in his own words) quotable rather than notable. Nevertheless, there are several unexpected novelties here, and more than a few important surprises.

The greatest surprise is the method. Ted Cott does not merely present his poems, he re-presents them. In a skillful and completely unorthodox approach, he supplements each poem with a revivifying interpretation. Each is a highly personal epilogue, and there are obvious dangers in it. But the tone is so free, the manner so fresh that the whole thing comes off brilliantly. Ted Cott's commentary is the touch, the trick, the angle—where's that radio thesaurus? Ah yes!—the gimmick which brings the separate segments into a unified program. His prose is not only a background but a challenge. And that is as it should be. For there never has been anything more fresh and challenging than the living, breathing—and breathless—spirit of poetry.

LOUIS UNTERMEYER

CONTENTS

PREFACE

A *Treasury of the Spoken Word* was undertaken in the Spring of 1948 at the invitation of Jack Kapp, President of Decca Records. The plan was to present familiar favorites in terms of their end product—reading aloud. The author was designated as director of the project, and the talents of three well-known actors, Raymond Edward Johnson, Jay Jostyn and Arnold Moss, were recruited.

The directions and interpretative background restated in this book are the same as those given to the three artists who made the transcriptions and records that are now at the service of schools and radio stations in the United States and Canada. The poems in this volume come chaperoned by the practical experience of this project. These poems were selected not because they are the most notable, but because they are the most quotable. In translating the written word into the spoken word, the author in his role as director found that the scene was most easily set by bringing into play the colloquialisms of present day activities. In this book, as in the studio, you will find references to football games, motion-picture techniques and modern-day equivalents to classical matters. Sir Walter Scott's Lochinvar is likened to Hop-a-long Cassidy in kilts; *The Raven* became *The Lost Weekend* set to rhyme; Polonius became a Shakespearean John J. Anthony.

The actors readily seized upon these images as an aid to the perspective of their readings. But matters of interpretation are subject to argument. In all probability, you will find some suggestions that do not match up with your conception. Certainly, then, this forms the first step toward deeper understanding. Even if you find yourself at odds with every analysis, we shall content ourselves in the knowledge that we have activated your personal interpretive gland.

The root of this project was planted in the soil of the program schedule of Radio Station WNEW, in New York. The furtherance of the project was dictated by the excellent and enthusiastic response to this initial radio series. At the end of this volume is appended a list of available dramatic material by well-known interpreters; these records were the broadcast units of the radio series. In many cases, you will find available identical pieces by different artists. The differences are indicative of the broad canvas on which the interpreter paints. With this anthology, you add *your* interpretation to those of the recording artists.

In starting to read these poems, remember that *you* sit at the head of the table of contents. The selections in this volume are not served by the editor as a literary butler. This is an anthology served buffet style. You are invited to take what you will. In collating the dishes, you will want to choose those that most please your palate.

Perhaps you will be a bit lost at first. Perhaps you've lost touch with Erato, the Muse of Poetry. It is true that until now poetry has been almost completely isolated in America's classrooms on literature. There it has become a hurdle in an obstacle race toward an academic degree. In schools one learns enough to pass an examination—but then one moves on to reading the sports pages and cheering or sneering the current favorites.

Maybe that is because students do not have enough chance to read poetry aloud, or to learn how to read it aloud. Maybe they never really learn the beauty of the spoken word.

In olden times, the poems would have died had they not been kept alive by the transfusions of the wandering minstrels

who set the words to music and passed them on from father
to son. That art has become obsolete, almost, except for a small
group of folk songs. But the poet, like the playwright, needs an
audience. The theatre has provided actors; the publishers of
poetry have provided anthologists, but no actors.

Where are the interpreters of rhyme? Where are the readers
of poetry? The performers will alibi their lack of interest by the
claim that poetry isn't commercial. Fine art is not "box office."
Yet Shakespeare managed to be the best box office attraction of
three hundred years, and his plays were poems. Perhaps the
reason why Americans today do not consider poetry "box office"
is that there is so little opportunity for poetry readers to partici-
pate in poetry. If we take an American activity that definitely
is "box office," that is, the great sport of baseball, we see that
although the average man would not dare to take over second
base in one of the big league games he can still learn the game
and play the game and love the game—as a member of a
sandlot team. Once his interest is developed through his amateur participation, he will of course go to the stadiums to watch
the pros. And that's why seventy thousand fans per game make
baseball "box office."

Radio has discovered that the injection of audience participation in a program has a nice effect on the program's Hooper
rating. When the poets can get enough mass acceptance to
warrant a Hooper rating instead of a Pulitzer prize, then we
shall see poetry fulfill its destiny, for the reading of a poem
glorifies its creation. It is the end product in the chain of the
poem's conception.

There have been few big time poetry readers on the air; a
result not from lack of interest, but from lack of opportunity.
But in the rare instances when poetry has been put on the air,
it has stood out as a prime radio ingredient. A. L. Alexander
had a program of poems; he announced that the sales managers
didn't think people were interested in poems, and from that

casual remark, drew more than twenty-thousand ballots of approval.

This volume is the coach of your "sandlot team," the "audience show" of poetry. It is on a simple scale of artistic interpretation. (Referring to our baseball parallel, it is fair to note that the man who pitched the World Series wouldn't have made it without the groundwork of his amateur standing.) Throughout, the emphasis is on the colloquial rather than on the classical. For by the integration of poems into the flow of modern-day living can we best bring these poems to life. Therefore, we say to you—you sit at the head of our table of contents. At this point, I'd like to tell you how we at WNEW marked the instructions for the actors on the poems they were to read, and also how you can adapt this system to your own reading needs.

There is more to turning the written word into the spoken word than clearing your throat.

Your vocal chords must be tied tight to your emotions.

To paraphrase an old saw and apply it to interpretation: ten percent inspiration, ninety percent perspiration.

Talent is not discovered; it is developed.

Talent is developed not like a photograph in the dark room with the aid of magical chemicals, but rather by the catalytic agent of experience. In any field where personal control is the deciding factor, practice, and only practice, makes perfect.

Performance is the channel of acquiring skill. Not necessarily public performance, for the mechanical age has brought electronics to the aid of the party. Tape, wire, and disc recorders are all excellent critical devices that give to the performer the double value of a voice mirror and the opportunity for the development of his self-critical gland.

The poems in this *Treasury of the Spoken Word* perform

double duty in the anthological field, presenting some familiar favorites under one roof as well as providing a starting post to their interpretation. As we have previously stated, these interpretations are there for you to follow or knock down as your own reaction dictates. Carbon paper is good for making duplicates, but true creative work forsakes the mimics and insists that each performance be an edition of one, limited and signed by the reader's own hand. All else is forgery and easily detected. Therefore, these clues and challenges must be considered a transient helping hand and not a permanent crutch.

As you put this book to use, you will find that certain modern conveniences have been built in. The foremost of these, at the insistence of Arthur Ceppos, President of the Hermitage domain, is the typographical set-up. Since these poems were meant for reading, large type has been used as a service to the eyes, and wider spaces in between lines as a service to your pencil. Yes, this is a book that is designed for marking up. Should this, despite Polonius' advice, be either borrowed or lent, we beg your forbearance in consideration of other borrowers and lenders. But once this book joins your personal library, we urge that you use it to the full.

When you settle on a poem that you want to work on, read it through first.

Then read it again.

Go through it a third time; this time slowly and deliberately.

Then, and only then, read the annotation.

Step five should bring you to the head of the work again. This time re-read the piece, applying the suggestions of the annotator. Exercise patience; a poem wasn't built in a day.

Challenge the annotator's remarks. Improve on them, disagree, perhaps, and build up your own foundation for interpretation.

After you have the conception of the work clearly in mind, start reading aloud. If the first run-through seems to jell, put your pencil to work. Interpretation is a series of changing notions erected on a constructed base. In achieving the end product of your basic conception, you will find that your techniques will change from reading to reading. You may perhaps change your plan of emphasis, turn away from your original pattern of pace changes.

Now you are ready to give yourself a more permanent guide sheet.

Your technique is not static; you will want to make changes. Therefore, make sure to use a soft lead in whatever pencilling device you choose. This makes for ready erasure. Any markings you make are a personal code to help you speak your piece. They are highly personal and in the long run you will probably develop your own shorthand system. As a starter, and for as much exercise as you wish to give them, we have organized a small dictionary of vocal punctuation, with examples, that may be helpful.

ACCENT

This will be used in connection with polysyllabic words in order to put the right emphasis on the right syllable. Consult your dictionary for pronunciation guides and for definitions.
Note that three different kinds of markings are used. Choose your weapon.

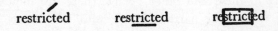

PAUSES

Here is the red light of vocal punctuation. Some readers have found it useful to actually use a soft red pencil for this task.

Others find the color change a psychological retard. Try both. Pauses, too, are of various durations and different symbols can be used to cure the variance. Thus, (**/**) after a word can be a short halt; (**|||**) a longer pause; and for a complete stop (**⌐**).

"With malice toward none **/**, with charity for all **/**, with firmness in the right as God gives us to see the right **/**, let us finish the work we are in **/**, to bind up the nation's wounds, to care for him who shall have borne the battle **/**, and for his widow and orphans **/**, to do all which we may achieve and cherish a just and lasting peace among ourselves **//** and with all nations. **⌐**

EMPHASIS

Emphasis on a particular word or phrase is hard to indicate since there is a great variety in the kind of emphasis you will want to apply. Thickness of your marking is one method of suggesting a degree of emphasis.

"With <u>malice</u> toward <u>none</u>, with <u>charity</u> for all, with <u>firmness</u> in the right as God <u>gives</u> us to <u>see the right</u> . . ."

CHARACTERIZING

Frequently in these and other poems, there are indications for switching from your narrator's role into the dialect or mannerism of a particular individual. It is good to mark these. A suggested manner is by boxing-off the characterized portion.

And he said, ⌐"The time has come I must admit."⌐

And then he added, ⌐"Let's get to the bottom of it."⌐

INFLECTIONS

Words, phrases, and sometimes sentences end on a rising note or a falling note. The big problem here is one of anticipation. It is almost impossible to achieve either effect without planning your reading to include it. Therefore, this marking must have a warning quality.

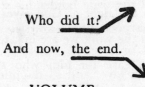

Who did it?

And now, the end.

VOLUME

Volume, on the whole, remains fairly constant for reasonable lengths of time. Therefore, the main problem in marking in this category is in change of volume. A hard underline (██████████████) indicates increased volume, and a wavy line (〰〰〰〰〰) a softer tone. It is good to cue these changes in advance by margin markings, using (∧) for up and (∨) for down.

And there's one other suggestion about marking up this book that you can use or not, depending on whether you think it will make things easier. Since in our guides to reading aloud, we very often refer to a specific line of a poem, it might be a good idea to number every fifth line with a small 1, 5, 10, 15, etc. at the end of the line, a little above the letters. Then, when a specific line is referred to, it won't be necessary to begin counting from the top each time. The numbers will also be a help in keeping track of pace changes.

On the following pages are a few samples taken from *A Treasury of the Spoken Word* and marked for reading. Study these, but do not necessarily follow them. As a broad rule, try to mark up a poem as little as possible. While these markings are a great help in the early stages of the genesis of your interpretation, they may act as an artificial device that will impede the forward motion of your reading.

LOCHINVAR

Sir Walter Scott

Oh, young Lochinvar is come out of the west: / 1.
Through all the wide border his steed was the best;
And save his good broadsword he weapons had none;
He rode all unarmed and he rode all alone. ||
So faithful in love, and so dauntless in war, 5.
There never was knight like the young Lochinvar!

He stayed not for brake, and he stopped not for stone;
He swam the Esk River where ford there was none: /
But ere he alighted at Netherby gate,
The bride had consented, the gallant came late; || 10.
For a laggard in love, and a dastard in war,
Was to wed the fair Ellen of brave Lochinvar.

So boldly he entered the Netherby Hall,
Among bridesmen, and kinsmen, and brothers, and all:
slow Then spoke the bride's father, his hand on his sword 15.
(For the poor craven bridegroom said never a word),
"O come ye in peace here, or come ye in war,
Or to dance at our bridal, young Lord Lochinvar?"

"I long wooed your daughter, my suit you denied;—
Love swells like the Solway, but ebbs like its tide!
And now am I come, with this lost love of mine,
To lead but one measure, drink one cup of wine:
There are maidens in Scotland more lovely by far,
That would gladly be bride to the young Lochinvar."

The bride kissed the goblet: the knight took it up,
He quaffed off the wine, and he threw down the cup.
She looked down to blush, and she looked up to sigh,
With a smile on her lips, and a tear in her eye.
He took her soft hand, ere her mother could bar,—
"Now tread we a measure!" said young Lochinvar.

So stately his form, and so lovely her face,
That never a hall such a galliard did grace:
While her mother did fret, and her father did fume,
And the bridegroom stood dangling his bonnet and
     plume;
And the bride-maidens whispered, " 'Twere better far
To have matched our fair cousin with young Loch-
     invar."

(. And so forth.)

Previously in this chapter we suggested the use of recording equipment for study. These few sentences are by way of a further endorsement and some additional suggestions for their use. The development in this field have been rapid; it is now possible to buy a home recorder for under fifty dollars and a professional type for a sum that runs in the neighborhood of a hundred dollars. The value of these devices is not so much to enable you to hear yourself as to allow you to criticize yourself. The finest readers are those who have the highest development of their self-critical abilities. After you make a record, or record yourself on wire or tape, play it back. Check your reading by following the words in print. There is a tendency to listen to yourself and move your lips unconsciously, mouthing not only each word but each mistake. But holding on the anchor of the original printed version, you are forced to set up a yardstick for comparison. Don't hesitate to play these records for your teachers or your friends. Pick out the understanding ones. Get their reactions, But don't destroy your record! It is more helpful to hear yourself six weeks later than six minutes after you first record. As you go on, these comparisons will inspire you and stimulate you for further work along these lines.

The poems in this volume are treated differently. Some have almost exact directions for pauses, emphasis and tempos. With others, the treatment is in broad terms. This has been purposely done. Getting yourself in the proper attitude for a particular piece, which is the intent of the general approach, is far more important than any mechanical contrivance. There are dramatic tricks which are arrived at after a series of local stops and not by direct express. These will come naturally. As you develop greater control over your elocutionary abilities, you will find yourself doing tricks of pace changing and emphasis that would have seemed impossible when you started. But with this technique as a starter, you can be your own anthologist. All that is needed is a book of blank pages, a scissors, some paste and a few old magazines or books that hold some of your favorites in escrow.

In telling you why this book *is,* and why it is the way it is, there's still one thing to talk about. I've already said that reading poetry aloud will give it a new and richer meaning. But I think you'll find it does something else. It will probably be the biggest ego-builder-upper in the world for you. It will probably do more to improve your confidence in yourself than you can possibly imagine.

As most people seem to know, hearing the sound of one's own voice is a very important thing. Witness the ultimate punishment of a recalcitrant gangster who is placed in "solitary" and emerges much easier to handle. Witness, also, the action of a small child (or a not-so-small-child) who whistles or carries on defiant conversation with the ghosts as he passes a moonlit, white-shadowed cemetery. And in a more pertinent vein, remember how carefully each budding politician or important statesman is coached in elocution, not so much to abet him in making speeches but primarily to give him confidence in facing his audience of voters. Debutantes are groomed as carefully in speaking as in picking a suitable husband; actors are given poems and speeches to learn long before they are ever taught to move downstage without tripping over stage sofas. (While you may not wind up with your name in lights, I think you'll enjoy this part, anyway, of an actor's training!)

Nowadays, when psychiatrists and psychoanalysts are stressing the need to "express yourself" they are very often recommending the reading aloud of poetry as an initial step, for it is said that nothing serves a nervous person so well as getting used to bringing his emotions out into the daylight of spoken words. And poetry is an excellent method for doing this, because no partner, no co-actor is necessary. One of my friends was recently advised to do this very thing to improve her self-confidence. She spoke to me about it and wailed, "Ted, I just don't know where to begin. I sit down every night with a great big thick book of poems and I start to read one and then another and then another, but it's so *hard*. I just make sing-song sounds and the poems sound so awful that it makes me feel more afraid than ever!"

Well, I think most people feel that way about reading poetry aloud. They'd love to—but they just don't know where to begin.

This book will serve, I hope, as their jumping-off point. It will show how to grasp the poet's idea behind whatever poem you choose to read as well as how to pick the poet's "cues" for the poem's interpretation. After that—the rest is a personal matter. For when once you've grasped the basic meaning and have also realized a few technical necessities in reading you will have the great fun of deciding yourself whether to pause or not to pause, to hurry or go slow, to act out a part or simply tell a story. Before long you'll have an unconquerable urge to read poetry aloud to your friends and I think you'll like the feel of the "spotlight" whether it be a real one or the one that a group of intent, admiring listeners cast with their watching eyes.

TED COTT

OVERTURE

Then read from the treasured volume

The poem of thy choice,

And lend to the rhyme of the poet

The beauty of thy voice.

LONGFELLOW

THE STAR-SPANGLED BANNER

Francis Scott Key

O say, can you see, by the dawn's early light,
  What so proudly we hailed at the twilight's last
    gleaming?
Whose broad stripes and bright stars, through the
    perilous fight,
  O'er the ramparts we watched, were so gallantly
    streaming!
And the rockets' red glare, the bombs bursting in air,
Gave proof through the night that our flag was still
    there:
  O say, does that star-spangled banner yet wave
  O'er the land of the free and the home of the brave?

On the shore, dimly seen through the mists of the deep,
  Where the foe's haughty host in dread silence reposes,
What is that which the breeze, o'er the towering steep,
  As it fitfully blows, now conceals, now discloses?
Now it catches the gleam of the morning's first beam,
In full glory reflected now shines on the stream:
  'Tis the star-spangled banner! O long may it wave
  O'er the land of the free and the home of the brave!

And where is that band who so vauntingly swore
　　That the havoc of war and the battle's confusion
A home and a country should leave us no more?
　　Their blood has washed out their foul footsteps'
　　　pollution.
No refuge could save the hireling and slave
From the terror of flight, or the gloom of the grave:
　　And the star-spangled banner in triumph doth wave
　　O'er the land of the free and the home of the brave!

Oh! thus be it ever, when freemen shall stand
　　Between their loved homes and the war's desolation!
Blest with victory and peace, may the heaven-rescued
　　land
　　Praise the Power that hath made and preserved us
　　　a nation.
Then conquer we must, for our cause it is just,
And this be our motto: "In God is our trust."
　　And the star-spangled banner in triumph shall wave
　　O'er the land of the free and the home of the brave!

By re-directing our thinking of "The Star-Spangled Banner" as our national anthem and placing it for a moment in the top drawer of war poems, we return the anthem to the scene of its creation and photograph a national symbol from a different angle by the use of a lens more appropriate to closeups than to panoramic views.

In the biography of this work, we start at its conception with the realization that it was written initially as a poem. It was later fitted to music and still later adopted as our national anthem. As our anthem, "The Star Spangled Banner" has become a one stanza poem; the other four are almost forgotten and remain unused except for reprinting in an occasional anthology, or as a quiz question on the radio. By treating it as a poem and tracing it to the point of origin, the first stanza stands beside its brothers and becomes a narrative documenting the bombardment of Fort McHenry by the British Navy. The story of its conception is a schoolboy "must," and need not be reprinted but only recalled. For it is from this perspective we urge its interpretation.

You are aboard a British battleship in 1814. Your name is Francis Scott Key. You are a lawyer who has visited the British Admiral on a mission to secure the release of a certain Dr. Beans. Because the British are about to attack Fort McHenry, you are not allowed to leave. Further, the Admiral has boasted that the Fort couldn't possibly hold out until daylight. All night you have vibrated with the rumbling of the cannon. Now the dawn has come. Eagerly you look out across the water. Is the flag still there? Has the fort surrendered? You peer through the early morning haze. Your heart accelerates its tempo. It's there! And now the guns are silent; it is quiet.

You turn to Dr. Beans, standing by your side, and ask, "Oh, say, can you see by the dawn's early light . . .?"

In reading this work as a poem, don't fall into the trap of musical tradition. As a poem you respect the comma after "say," whereas the song runs the words "Oh say can you see" together. When you reach the word "proof," underscore it. By emphasizing this word a natural pause will result and strengthen the preceding and following phrases.

Again in the second stanza, watch the commas. Pause after "shore." When you reach the fourth line, become a radio announcer at the event. When you read the line "now conceals, now discloses," react to it exactly as you would if you were actually seeing it appear and disappear. At the point of discovery—"Tis the Star-Spangled Banner"—build up to a climax. Then, pause at the end of this stanza.

The third stanza calls for a new tack. This is the sweetest part of victory; you are gloating over your ability to throw back the vain boast of the British Admiral.

The last stanza is an affirmation of justice. Remember that Key was a lawyer. This is his closing address to the jury. He has won his case. He is sure of the decision and he thanks the Judge. Don't be dramatic in this stanza. Key is sure of himself. He speaks quietly. Make sure that you speak the words "when free men shall stand between their loved homes and the war's desolation" in one breath.

By transporting yourself to the deck of the British warship, and *being* Key, you will find new values in our national anthem.

THE GETTYSBURG ADDRESS
Abraham Lincoln

Fourscore and seven years ago
Our fathers brought forth on this continent
A new nation;
Conceived in liberty
And dedicated to the proposition:
That all men are created equal.

Now
We are engaged in a great civil war,
Testing whether that nation
or any nation
so conceived
And so dedicated
Can long endure.

We are met
On a great battlefield of that war.
We have come
To dedicate a portion of that field
As a final resting place
For those who here gave their lives
That this nation might live.

It is altogether fitting and proper
That we should do this.

But in a larger sense
We cannot dedicate
We cannot consecrate
We cannot hallow
   This ground

The brave men
   Living and dead
      Who struggled here
Have consecrated it.
Far above our poor powers
   To add or detract.

The world
Will little note
            Nor long remember
What we say here,
But it can never forget what they did
Here.

It is for us—the living
      Rather
To be dedicated here to the unfinished work
Which they who fought here

Have thus far
  Nobly advanced.

It is rather for us
  To be here dedicated
To the great task remaining before us—

That from these
  Honored Dead
We take increased devotion
  To that cause
For which they gave the last full measure
Of devotion.
That we here
Highly resolve
That these dead
    Shall not have died in vain;

That this nation
Under God
Shall have a new birth of freedom;
And
That government
    Of the people
    By the people
    For the people
Shall not perish from the earth.

HERE is the written word specifically intended to become the spoken word. It is frequent that a poem is written to be read at a dedication. But here is the occasional miracle—a speech that is really a poem. In these days journalistic ethics forbid a direct quotation of anything said by a President of the United States (other than his formal speeches). But we are certain that the poet who was the President of this country almost one hundred years ago would approve the liberty we take of reproducing his words in blank verse. The justification is inherent in the poem.

Several poems of Lincoln exist. And while this Gettysburg Address has more reason than rhyme, it is full of the rhythms that make for poetic expression.

It is fair to take this piece away from the speaker's podium at Gettysburg, and treat it as a collateral document to the Constitution and the Declaration of Independence. This is a mood piece of humility, in which Lincoln spoke not *to* the dead of Gettysburg but *for* them. For many years, this work has been a prime favorite of the textbooks; it was not too long for the average student to memorize—much easier to repeat than the constitution, simpler than the Declaration. It was not until ten years ago, when Charles Laughton interpolated a reading of this masterpiece into a motion picture called *Ruggles of Red Gap,* that it was claimed out of the pawn shops of the elocutionists. For his reading showed it again to be so loaded with overpowering emotion that the Address was rediscovered as a poem.

Commentators at the time noted that it was almost paradoxically an Englishman, with an English accent, who revived the magnificence of a mid-westerner's psalm of democracy. At

the drop of a stove-pipe hat Raymond Massey, the most famous
of the Lincoln interpreters, will recite this poem. Not in any
way to deprecate his performance, it is vital to realize that
Massey reads this poem *as* Lincoln. It is our recommendation
that it develops its greatest validity and application when it
is read by any American person as a testament of his faith.

In printing the Gettysburg Address in the mould of poetry,
we have been able to eliminate a great many otherwise necessary directions for the reading. The phrasing is easily understood by this form. For the actual mood, we infringe on our
own copyright and reiterate a sentence made earlier in this
analysis: Lincoln was speaking *for* the dead of Gettysburg,
not *to* them. This is a triumph of faith, not a dirge of memorial.
Your reading should be quiet, but not sad.

THE TWENTY-THIRD PSALM

(*From The Book of Psalms*)

The Lord is my shepherd; I shall not want.

He maketh me to lie down in green pastures;

He leadeth me beside the still waters.

He restoreth my soul;

He leadeth me in the paths of righteousness for his
name's sake.

Yea, though I walk through the valley of the shadow
of death,

I will fear no evil: for thou art with me;

Thy rod and thy staff they comfort me.

Thou preparest a table before me in the presence of
mine enemies;

Thou anointest my head with oil; my cup runneth over.

Surely goodness and mercy shall follow me all the days
of my life,

And I will dwell in the house of the Lord forever.

THE Psalms of David have a unique place in this anthology. Through their centuries of use, they realize their point only upon vocal and spiritual adoption by the reader. Too often are the psalms read *at* you instead of by *you*. They are highly personalized prayers. The twenty-third in the series is the most quoted. The simplicity of the symbolism (the Lord is my shepherd) is the keynote to the reading. The author *was* a shepherd, knows the care he lavished on his flock and has chosen this symbolism to represent the Deity. In Molnar's play "Liliom" the leading player dies and goes to a heaven of his own imagination. There he conceives of God as the judge of the police court with which his various troubles with the law had brought him into contact. It is interesting to realize the images of the Deity which men and women create to represent their reverence. This fact is relevent to the interpretation, for it is only by personal conviction that these works can be vital.

In the first five lines, all the verbs must be emphasized. This refers to "maketh," "leadeth," "restoreth." The "Yea" is read as though it were "Ah, yes!"; draw it out; hover over this word. Note, too, that each sentence can stand alone and be a complete thought. Read it quietly, softly, deeply (both in voice and emotion).

POLONIUS' ADVICE TO HIS SON
William Shakespeare

These few precepts in thy memory
See thou character. Give thy thoughts no tongue,
Nor any unproportion'd thought his act.
Be thou familiar, but by no means vulgar:
The friends thou hast, and their adoption tried,
Grapple them to thy soul with hoops of steel;
But do not dull thy palm with entertainment
Of each new-hatch'd, unfledg'd comrade. Beware
Of entrance to a quarrel: but being in,
Bear't that th' opposed may beware of thee.
Give every man thine ear, but few thy voice:
Take each man's censure, but reserve thy judgment.
Costly thy habit as thy purse can buy,
But not express'd in fancy: rich, not gaudy;
For the apparel oft proclaims the man.
Neither a borrower nor a lender be;
For loan oft loses both itself and friend,
And borrowing dulls the edge of husbandry.
This above all: to thine own self be true;
And it must follow, as the night the day,
Thou canst not then be false to any man.

(from HAMLET)

PLAYED in character, Polonius is traditionally etched by actors as a doddering old fool. Yet the lines entrusted to him by Shakespeare are not the advice of a fool. The precepts are so valuable, so penetrating that when they are taken from the context of the play, they shape themselves into a poem. Let us rather think of Polonius as a Shakespearean John J. Anthony. Laying aside the traditional characterization of Polonius, we have laid the cornerstone for a fresh approach to the reading of this piece.

In the actual reading, it will be advisable to be at once warm and persuasive. Treat each item of advice as a unit. In the third line from the end of this extract, a change of tone is called for. The advice turns from the specific to the general. "To thine own self be true" must carry with it a sincerity that has overtones of the spiritual as contrasted to the previous inventory of suggestions which are clues to practical matters.

RIVALS

William Walsh

Of all the torments, all the cares,
　With which our lives are cursed;
Of all the plagues a lover bears,
　Sure rivals are the worst!
By partners in each other kind
　Afflictions easier grow;
In love alone we hate to find
　Companions of our woe.

Sylvia, for all the pangs you see
　Are laboring in my breast,
I beg not you would favor me,
　Would you but slight the rest!
How great soe'er your rigors are,
　With them alone I'll cope;
I can endure my own despair,
　But not another's hope.

THE idea that jealousy is a splinter of hate is aptly epito-
mized in "Rivals." This lover is the kind that murders a girl
rather than have another marry her. This piece is usually
placed amongst the words of the Cavalier poets, who celebrate
Valentine's Day three hundred and sixty-five times a year; and
with another valentine as often as possible. This man has
received a tentative nomination; he is disturbed at waiting so
long for election. By specifically personalizing the poem, and
mentioning the lady by name, he is attempting a romantic
argument. But taking the poem in a broader sense, we cannot
feel the sympathy for him that he intends his poem to arouse
in the heart of Sylvia. So take this poem in the manner of
your choosing. You can make it a charming love letter, or
you can treat it as an unstable declaration of insecurity. This
man is more in love with himself than with the young lady.

Of course the lady will be sure to respond to so gallant
a charge, but will soon learn to differentiate between today's
infatuation and tomorrow's love. You may read this as a light
demonstration of love, or as a mood piece of frustration. On
the one hand you can breeze through the work. On the other
you will want to read it slower, with intensity. In the first
interpretation, for example, the word "cursed" in the first
stanza is just one word among many to be slurred over for an
overall effect. In the second reading, you underscore this word,
etch it with bitterness.

Here is an interesting Dr. Jekyll and Mr. Hyde possibility.
Read the poem both ways and decide on the one you like
better.

WOODMAN, SPARE THAT TREE
George P. Morris

Woodman, spare that tree!
Touch not a single bough!
In youth it sheltered me,
And I'll protect it now.
'Twas my forefather's hand
That placed it near his cot;
There, woodman, let it stand
Thy ax shall harm it not!

That old familiar tree,
Whose glory and renown
Are spread o'er land and sea,
And wouldst thou hew it down?

Woodman, forbear thy stroke!
Cut not its earth-bound ties!
Oh! spare that aged oak,
Now towering to the skies.

When but an idle boy
I sought its grateful shade;
In all their gushing joy
Here too my sisters played.

My mother kissed me here
My father pressed my hand—
Forgive this foolish tear,
But let that old oak stand!

My heart-strings round thee cling,
Close as thy bark, old friend!
Here shall the wild-bird sing,
And still thy branches bend.
Old tree, the storm still brave!
And, woodman, leave the spot!
While I've a hand to save,
Thy ax shall harm it not.

SERIOUSLY speaking, and it's an effort in this case, here is a tenth-rate poem that should be properly indexed in your laughter file. To present this piece in its intended shape will cause you to work up an emotional sweat over a comparatively unimportant matter. Since we have so often in our annotation of this anthology stressed the importance of reading these poems in terms of contemporary techniques and backdrops, we find it hard to urge you to raise your voice in defence of a tree when there are so many more important matters that require your eloquence. Because it is an old favorite, and has been a frequent visitor on the stages of the high school elocutionists of the past fifty years, we felt obligated to let it show its face. This, like Ten Nights in a Barroom, was played in dead earnest for decades. But now, like that play on temperance, it is a fit companion for pretzels and beer. Rather than have your listeners laugh at you, beat them to the punch. Laugh your way through it. Such phrases as "When but an idle boy," "Close as thy bark, old friend," "Oh, spare that aged oak," "Woodman, forbear thy stroke" will make it an easy task. This poem has become its own satire. The leaves have fallen off, and the only alternative is to tell the woodman to go ahead and help him swing the ax.

THE FACE ON THE FLOOR

Hugh D'Arcy

'Twas a balmy summer evening, and a goodly crowd
    was there,
Which well-nigh filled Joe's bar-room, on the corner of
    the square;
And as songs and witty stories came through the open
    door,
A vagabond crept slowly in and posed upon the floor.

"Where did it come from?" someone said. "The wind
    has blown it in."
"What does it want?" another cried. "Some whiskey,
    rum or gin?"
"Here, Toby, seek 'em, if your stomach's equal to the
    work—
I wouldn't touch him with a fork, he's filthy as a Turk."

This badinage the poor wretch took with stoical good
    grace;
In fact, he smiled as tho' he thought he'd struck the
    proper place.
"Come, boys, I know there's kindly hearts among so
    good a crowd—
To be in such good company would make a deacon
    proud."

"Give me a drink—that's what I want—I'm out of
     funds, you know,
When I had the cash to treat the gang this hand was
     never slow.
What? You laugh as if you thought this pocket never
     held a sou;
I once was fixed as well, my boys, as any one of you."

"There, thanks, that's braced me nicely; God bless you
     one and all;
Next time I pass this good saloon I'll make another
     call.
Give you a song? No, I can't do that; my singing
     days are past;
My voice is cracked, my throat's worn out, and my
     lungs are going fast.

"Say! Give me another whiskey, and I'll tell you
     what I'll do—
I'll tell you a funny story, and a fact, I promise, too,
That ever I was a decent man not one of you would
     think;
But I was, some four or five years back. Say, give me
     another drink.

"Fill her up, Joe, I want to put some life into my
frame—
Such little drinks to a bum like me are miserably tame;
Five fingers—there, that's the scheme—and corking
whiskey, too.
Well, here's luck, boys, and landlord, my best regards
to you.

"You've treated me pretty kindly and I'd like to tell
you how
I came to be the dirty sot you see before you now.
As I told you, once I was a man, with muscle, frame
and health,
And, but for a blunder ought to have made consider-
able wealth.

"I was a painter—not one that daubed on bricks and
wood,
But an artist, and for my age, was rated pretty good.
I worked hard at my canvas, and was bidding fair
to rise,
For gradually I saw the star of fame before my eyes.

"I made a picture perhaps you've seen, 'tis called the
    'Chase of Fame.'
It brought me fifteen hundred pounds and added to
    my name.
And then I met a woman—now comes the funny part—
With eyes that petrified my brain, and sunk into my
    heart.

"Why don't you laugh? 'Tis funny that the vagabond
    you see
Could ever love a woman, and expect her love for me;
But 'twas so, and for a month or two, her smiles were
    freely given,
And when her loving lips touched mine, it carried me
    to heaven.

"Boys, did you ever see a girl for whom your soul
    you'd give,
With a form like the Milo Venus, too beautiful to live;
With eyes that would beat the Koh-i-noor, and a
    wealth of chestnut hair?
If so, 'twas she, for there never was another half so fair.

"I was working on a portrait, one afternoon in May,
Of a fair-haired boy, a friend of mine, who lived across
  the way;
And Madeline admired it, and, much to my surprise,
She said she'd like to know the man that had such
  dreamy eyes.

"It didn't take long to know him, and before the month
  had flown
My friend had stole my darling, and I was left alone;
And ere a year of misery had passed above my head,
The jewel I had treasured so had tarnished and was
  dead.

"That's why I took to drink, boys. Why, I never saw
  you smile,
I thought you'd be amused, and laughing all the while.
Why, what's the matter, friend? There's a tear-drop in
  your eye,
Come, laugh like me; 'tis only babes and women that
  should cry.

"Say, boys, if you give me just another whiskey I'll be
    glad,
And I'll draw right here a picture of the face that
    drove me mad.
Give me that piece of chalk with which you mark the
    baseball score—
You shall see the lovely Madeline upon the bar-room
    floor."

Another drink, and with chalk in hand, the vagabond
    began
To sketch a face that might well buy the soul of any
    man.
Then, as he placed another lock upon the shapely head,
With a fearful shriek, he leaped and fell across the
    picture—dead.

"THE Face on the Floor" is a real challenge to a competent reader. Your audience will parallel the reactions of the occupants of the bar when you start. They will be derisive, and perhaps if they're blessed with politeness will cover their smirks with their hands. But corny as this piece is, it can win you a round of applause by proper reading. As you read the work through you noted that after making fun of the artist, the scoffers bought him a drink. But when he started to narrate his story, they settled down to silence and sympathy. That's your job, too. Starting with the fourth stanza, the reader becomes the artist; picture him well and alcoholize your reading. (This is an interpretative directive and not an invitation to insobriety). In the first three stanzas you are the audience. The intriguing part of this work for you as the reader is that you protect yourself from your audience by being one of them. You anticipate their reaction to your reading by saying it *for* them. When they think, "Where did *it* come from," they're thinking about the poem, but you're setting up the artist.

The first three stanzas require a broad reading. In the second, break the strict rhythm of the piece and pull into your voice all the derisive quality you can. Sneer at the artist. Underline "It." Make him sound horrible when he is described "As dirty as a Turk."

At the third line of the third stanza, take on the role of the artist. He is a confirmed alcoholic, has a whiskey whisper. He's not a rolling drunk, unaware of what he's doing. This is his natural state. He slurs his words and his thoughts. Yet throughout he is shrewd; he knows how to tease his audience to get another slug of whiskey. His is an alcoholic cunning. And remember, each time he drinks you will have to thicken your voice. Keep your voice down. This isn't a noisy drunkard.

In the third stanza he wheedles the audience. At the end of the fourth stanza either make the sound or gesture of tossing a drink down. At the end of the second line of the fifth stanza take a pause to hear the unheard question of one of the saloon frequenters who asks for a song. You have decided to use this as a wedge for getting another drink. So lead into it gradually. You are willing to make a bargain, the most humiliating kind in the world: you are going into a confession box in a saloon. In the seventh stanza follow the physical actions detailed. Go through all the motions. Make this as natural as you can.

In the tenth stanza when you reach the third line, and introduce the woman, drop some of the drunken quality in your delivery. Start reading more slowly. Your voice becomes clearer: you are not the drunk, but the original artist reliving the unhappiness of the incident you describe.

The second stanza from the end, you are once again the man in the grip of alcohol. He is shrewdly appraising the situation to see if he can wheedle another drink.

In the last stanza, you leave him and once again become the voice of the audience. This time, affected by his story, you are quieter, slower. Don't overdo the dramatics of the situation. Read this stanza simply.

SONG

John Suckling

Why so pale and wan, fond lover?
   Prithee, why so pale?
Will, when looking well can't move her,
   Looking ill prevail?
   Prithee, why so pale?

Why so dull and mute, young sinner?
   Prithee, why so mute?
Will, when speaking well can't win her,
   Saying nothing do't?
   Prithee, why so mute?

Quit, quit, for shame, this will not move:
   This cannot take her.
If of herself she will not love,
   Nothing can make her:
   The devil take her!

from AGLAURA

HERE is a poem of comfort. An older, experienced lover is giving words of advice to a younger, experiencing lover. He realizes that in all cases where a lover's knot has slipped, it is always most comforting to place the blame on the opposite sex. The man of experience has a hard job; he is trying to bring logic to an illogical situation. His last line admits it.

The best effect from this piece is obtained by playing the role of the big brother. Treat the uncomfortable suitor almost as though he were a baby. Your tone approximates that of the father who, approached by a young son who has just banged his finger with a heavy hammer, solicitously informs him, "Oh, it doesn't hurt." Use your most soothing voice.

Keep this style throughout the piece until after the fourth line in the third stanza. Take a complete stop. Then harden your voice, as if recalling a similar situation you have gone through, and throw the lady in question to the winds. This is an amusing effect resulting from your serious attempt to straighten the matter out and then suddenly admitting that this is no way to deal with an unresponsive woman.

THE DIVERTING HISTORY
OF JOHN GILPIN

SHOWING HOW HE WENT FARTHER THAN HE INTENDED AND
CAME SAFE HOME AGAIN

William Cowper

John Gilpin was a citizen
   Of credit and renown,
A train-band captain eke was he
   Of famous London town.

John Gilpin's spouse said to her dear,
   "Though wedded we have been
These twice ten tedious years, yet we
   No holiday have seen.

"To-morrow is our wedding-day,
   And we will then repair
Unto the Bell at Edmonton,
   All in a chaise and pair.

"My sister, and my sister's child,
   Myself, and children three,
Will fill the chaise; so you must ride
   On horseback after we."

He soon replied, "I do admire
  Of womankind but one,
And you are she, my dearest dear,
  Therefore it shall be done.

"I am a linen-draper bold,
  As all the world doth know,
And my good friend the calender
  Will lend his horse to go."

Quoth Mrs. Gilpin, "That's well said;
  And for that wine is dear,
We will be furnished with our own,
  Which is both bright and clear."

John Gilpin kissed his loving wife;
  O'erjoyed was he to find,
That though on pleasure she was bent,
  She had a frugal mind.

The morning came, the chaise was brought,
  But yet was not allowed
To drive up to the door, lest all
  Should say that she was proud.

So three doors off the chaise was stayed,
  Where they did all get in;
Six precious souls, and all agog
  To dash through thick and thin.

Smack went the whip, round went the wheels,
  Were never folk so glad,
The stones did rattle underneath,
  As if Cheapside were mad.

John Gilpin at his horse's side
  Seized fast the flowing mane,
And up he got, in haste to ride,
  But soon came down again;

For saddle-tree scarce reached had he,
  His journey to begin,
When, turning round his head, he saw
  Three customers come in.

So down he came; for loss of time,
  Although it grieved him sore,
Yet loss of pence, full well he knew,
  Would trouble him much more.

'Twas long before the customers
  Were suited to their mind,
When Betty screaming came downstairs,
  "The wine is left behind!"

"Good lack!" quoth he—"yet bring it me,
  My leathern belt likewise,
In which I bear my trusty sword,
  When I do exercise."

Now Mistress Gilpin (careful soul!)
    Had two stone bottles found,
To hold the liquor that she loved,
    And keep it safe and sound.

Each bottle had a curling ear,
    Through which the belt he drew,
And hung a bottle on each side,
    To make his balance true.

Then over all, that he might be
    Equipped from top to toe,
His long red cloak, well brushed and neat,
    He manfully did throw.

Now see him mounted once again
    Upon his nimble steed,
Full slowly pacing o'er the stones,
    With caution and good heed.

But finding soon a smoother road
    Beneath his well-shod feet,
The snorting beast began to trot,
    Which galled him in his seat.

So, "Fair and softly," John he cried,
    But John he cried in vain;
That trot became a gallop soon,
    In spite of curb and rein.

So stooping down, as needs he must
    Who cannot sit upright,
He grasped the mane with both his hands,
    And eke with all his might.

His horse, who never in that sort
    Had handled been before,
What thing upon his back had got
    Did wonder more and more.

Away went Gilpin, neck or naught;
    Away went hat and wig:
He little dreamt, when he set out,
    Of running such a rig.

The wind did blow, the cloak did fly,
    Like streamer long and gay,
Till, loop and button failing both,
    At last it flew away.

Then might all people well discern
    The bottles he had slung;
A bottle swinging at each side,
    As hath been said or sung.

The dogs did bark, the children screamed,
    Up flew the windows all;
And every soul cried out, "Well done!"
    As loud as he could bawl.

Away went Gilpin—who but he?
　His fame soon spread around;
"He carries weight!" "He rides a race!"
　" 'Tis for a thousand pound!"

And still, as fast as he drew near,
　'Twas wonderful to view,
How in a trice the turnpike-men
　Their gates wide open threw.

And now, as he went bowing down
　His reeking head full low,
The bottles twain behind his back
　Were shattered at a blow.

Down ran the wine into the road,
　Most piteous to be seen,
Which made his horse's flanks to smoke
　As they had basted been.

But still he seemed to carry weight,
　With leathern girdle braced;
For all might see the bottle-necks
　Still dangling at his waist.

Thus all through merry Islington
　These gambols he did play,
Until he came unto the Wash
　Of Edmonton so gay;

And there he threw the Wash about
    On both sides of the way,
Just like unto a trundling mop,
    Or a wild goose at play.

At Edmonton his loving wife
    From the balcony spied
Her tender husband, wondering much
    To see how he did ride.

"Stop, stop, John Gilpin!—Here's the house!"
    They all at once did cry;
"The dinner waits, and we are tired;"—
    Said Gilpin—"So am I."

But yet his horse was not a whit
    Inclined to tarry there!
For why?—his owner had a house
    Full ten miles off, at Ware,

So like an arrow swift he flew,
    Shot by an archer strong;
So did he fly—which brings me to
    The middle of my song.

Away went Gilpin, out of breath,
    And sore against his will,
Till at his friend the calender's
    His horse at last stood still.

The calender, amazed to see
  His neighbor in such trim,
Laid down his pipe, flew to the gate,
  And thus accosted him:

"What news? what news? your tidings tell;
  Tell me you must and shall—
Say why bareheaded you are come,
  Or why you come at all?"

Now Gilpin had a pleasant wit
  And loved a timely joke;
And thus unto the calender
  In merry guise he spoke:

"I came because your horse would come,
  And, if I well forbode,
My hat and wig will soon be here.—
  They are upon the road."

The calender, right glad to find
  His friend in merry pin,
Returned him not a single word
  But to the house went in;

Whence straight he came with hat and wig;
  A wig that flowed behind,
A hat not much the worse for wear,
  Each comely in its kind.

He held them up, and in his turn
  Thus showed his ready wit,
"My head is twice as big as yours,
  They therefore needs must fit.

"But let me scrape the dirt away
  That hangs upon your face;
And stop and eat, for well you may
  Be in a hungry case."

Said John, "It is my wedding-day,
  And all the world would stare,
If wife should dine at Edmonton,
  And I should dine at Ware."

So turning to his horse, he said,
  "I am in haste to dine;
'Twas for your pleasure you came here,
  You shall go back for mine."

Ah, luckless speech, and bootless boast!
  For which he paid full dear;
For, while he spake, a braying ass
  Did sing most loud and clear;

Whereat his horse did snort, as he
  Had heard a lion roar,
And galloped off with all his might,
  As he had done before.

Away went Gilpin, and away
  Went Gilpin's hat and wig:
He lost them sooner than at first;
  For why?—they were too big.

Now Mistress Gilpin, when she saw
  Her husband posting down
Into the country far away,
  She pulled out half-a-crown;

And thus unto the youth she said
  That drove them to the Bell,
"This shall be yours, when you bring back
  My husband safe and well."

The youth did ride, and soon did meet
  John coming back amain:
Whom in a trice he tried to stop,
  By catching at his rein;

But not performing what he meant,
  And gladly would have done,
The frighted steed he frighted more,
  And made him faster run.

Away went Gilpin, and away
  Went postboy at his heels,
The postboy's horse right glad to miss
  The lumbering of the wheels.

Six gentlemen upon the road,
  Thus seeing Gilpin fly,
With postboy scampering in the rear,
  They raised the hue and cry:

"Stop thief! stop thief!—a highwayman!"
  Not one of them was mute;
And all and each that passed that way
  Did join in the pursuit.

And now the turnpike gates again
  Flew open in short space;
The toll-men thinking, as before,
  That Gilpin rode a race.

And so he did, and won it too,
  For he got first to town;
Nor stopped till where he had got up
  He did again get down.

Now let us sing, Long live the king!
  And Gilpin, long live he!
And when he next doth ride abroad
  May I be there to see!

IF THERE were only a part for Bing Crosby, this poem could easily be turned into one of those "Road" pictures with Bob Hope as John Gilpin—"The Road to Edmonton." Here is slapstick comedy and rowdy humor full of pit falls and misadventure. On second thought, and for the second generation, let's cast Harold Lloyd in the part.

When poetry is used as a vehicle for comedy, the usual injunction to run away from the rhyming patterns calls for a temporary veto. The fun derives from the emphasis on the rhymes. Then, too, the reading can be as broad as you like. Take the fifth verse: the florid flattery of Mr. Gilpin has none of the subtlety of the Cavalier poets. Mr. Gilpin is more at home with a baseball bat than with a rapier.

This piece is a series of snapshots. Therefore, do not concern yourself with the tying together of the various "stills." You are the narrator who is constantly discovering Mr. Gilpin in odd and assorted poses. Play it for laughs and you are permitted to laugh *at* Mr. Gilpin. You will find it pleasant to chuckle through some of his predicaments. Of course, this is a long piece. The problem of pacing yourself is more comparable to a cross-country run than to an hundred yard dash. You can't ever afford to go too fast, or too slow. But you will speed up in spurts to match the action.

We have heard this piece performed with an English cockney accent. If you do well at that sort of vocal manipulation, by all means proceed. But proceed at your own risk. If it isn't constant throughout you will find yourself in a misadventure capable of a Gilpin.

Mr. Gilpin is a man with two left feet and while you are not taking on his role, you develop a good slice of humor by being amused by him. William Cowper has a bit of the Damon Runyon in him.

MAUD MULLER

John Greenleaf Whittier

Maud Muller on a summer's day
Raked the meadow sweet with hay.

Beneath her torn hat glowed the wealth
Of simple beauty and rustic health.

Singing, she wrought, and her merry glee
The mock-bird echoed from his tree.

But when she glanced to the far-off town,
White from its hill-slope looking down,
The sweet song died,

And a vague unrest
And a nameless longing filled her breast,—
A wish that she hardly dared to own,
For something better than she had known.

The Judge rode slowly down the lane,
Smoothing his horse's chestnut mane.
He drew his bridle in the shade
Of the apple-trees, to greet the maid.
And asked a draught from the spring that flowed
Through the meadow across the road.

She stooped where the cool spring bubbled up,
And filled for him her small tin cup,
And blushed as she gave it, looking down
On her feet so bare, and her tattered gown.

"Thanks!" said the Judge; "a sweeter draught
From a fairer hand was never quaffed."

He spoke of the grass and flowers and trees,
Of the singing birds and the humming bees;
Then talked of the haying, and wondered whether
The cloud in the west would bring foul weather.
And Maud forgot her brier-torn gown,
And her graceful ankles bare and brown;
And listened while a pleased surprise
Looked from her long-lashed hazel eyes.

At last, like one who for delay
Seeks a vain excuse, he rode away.

Maud Muller looked and sighed: "Ah me!
That I the Judge's bride might be!
He would dress me up in silks so fine,
And praise and toast me at his wine.
My father should wear a broadcloth coat;
My brother should sail a painted boat,
I'd dress my mother so grand and gay,

And the baby should have a new toy each day.
And I'd feed the hungry and clothe the poor,
And all should bless me who left our door."

The Judge looked back as he climbed the hill,
And saw Maud Muller standing still.
"A form more fair, a face more sweet,
Ne'er hath it been my lot to meet.
And her modest answer and graceful air
Show her wise and good as she is fair,
"Would she were mine, and I today,
Like her, a harvester of hay;
No doubtful balance of rights and wrongs,
Nor weary lawyers with endless tongues,
But low of cattle and song of birds,
And health and quiet and loving words."

But he thought of his sisters, proud and cold,
And his mother, vain of her rank and gold.
So, closing his heart, the Judge rode on,
And Maud was left in the field alone.

But the lawyers smiled that afternoon,
When he hummed in court an old love-tune;

And the young girl mused beside the well
Til the rain on the unraked clover fell.

He wedded a wife of richest dower,

Who lived for fashion, as he for power.

Yet oft, in his marble hearth's bright flow,

He watched a picture come and go;

And sweet Maud Muller's hazel eyes

Looked out in their innocent surprise.

Oft, when the wine in his glass was red,

He longed for the wayside well instead;

And closed his eyes on his garnished rooms

To dream of meadows and clover-blooms.

And the proud man sighed, with a secret pain,

"Ah, that I were free again!

Free as when I rode that day,

Where the barefoot maiden raked her hay."

She wedded a man unlearned and poor,

And many children played round her door.

But care and sorrow, and childbirth pain,

Left their traces on heart and brain.

And oft, when the summer sun shone hot

On the new-mown hay in the meadow lot,

And she heard the little spring brook fall

Over the roadside, through the wall,

In the shade of the apple tree again

She saw a rider draw his rein;

And gazing down with timid grace,

She felt his pleased eyes read her face.

Sometimes her narrow kitchen walls
Stretched away into stately halls;
The weary wheel to a spinet turned,
The tallow candle an astral burned,
And for him who sat by the chimney lug,
Dozing and grumbling o'er pipe and mug,
A manly form at her side she saw,
And joy was duty and love was law.
Then she took up her burden of life again,
Saying only, "It might have been."

Alas for maiden, alas for Judge,
For rich repiner and household drudge.
God pity them both! and pity us all,
Who vainly the dreams of youth recall.
For of all sad words of tongue or pen,
The saddest are these: "It might have been!"

Ah, well! for us all some sweet hope lies
Deeply buried from human eyes;
And in the hereafter, angels may
Roll the stone from its grave away!

IN HIS definitive anthology, Burton Stevenson lists this piece amongst the poems of Love. To write off the Judge and Maud as two lovers is to do a disservice to the poet's intentions. This is not a love poem, but rather an exploration of frustration. Neither Maud nor the Judge were in love with each other. They were unhappy with themselves and their casual meeting symbolized only the possibility of escape; they were not prisoners of their environment, but rather prisoners of themselves. Cursing the jailer never got anybody a reprieve.

Maud Muller is a fable. The two stars are illustrative of a problem, which Whittier resolves in the last five paragraphs. Maud and the Judge are as symbolic as the Fox and the Grapes or the Lion and the Mouse in Mr. Aesop's table of fables. Therefore, in reading this work, don't overdo the descriptive passages. Miss Muller and the Judge are not valuable to the story because of any particular virtue, but rather because of their weaknesses. By leaning on the characterizations of their appearance, you will draw sympathy for them and dilute the moral.

As far as the actual reading is concerned, you may have a tendency to get a staccato effect if you follow the original two line stanza architecture of this work.

Therefore, the annotator has taken the liberty of marrying some of the stanzas to make the reading easier. This is not revocation of poet's license, but rather a concession to dramatic expediency.

THE KID'S LAST FIGHT

Anonymous

Us two was pals, the Kid and me;
'Twould cut no ice if some gayzee,
As tough as nails jumped either one,
We'd both light in and hand him some.

We were the same size, the Kid and me,
We tipped the scales at thirty-three;
And when we'd spar 'twas give and take,
I wouldn't slug for any stake.

One day we worked out at the gym,
Some swell guy hangin' round called "Slim,"
Watched us and got stuck on the Kid,
Then signed him up, that's what he did.

This guy called "Slim" he owned a string
Of lightweights, welters, everything;
He took the Kid out on the road,
And where they went none of us knowed.

I guessed the Kid had changed his name,
And fightin' the best ones in the game.
I used to dream of him at night,
No letters came—he couldn't write.

In just about two months or three
I signed up with Bucktooth McGee.
He got me matched with Denver Brown,
I finished him in half a round.

Next month I fought with Brooklyn Mike,
As tough a boy who hit the pike;
Then Frisco Jim and Battlin' Ben,
And knocked them all inside of ten.

I took 'em all and won each bout,
None of them birds could put me out;
The sportin' writers watched me slug,
Then all the papers run my mug.

"He'd rather fight than eat," they said,
"He's got the punch, he'll knock 'em dead."
There's only one I hadn't met,
That guy they called "The Yorkshire Pet."

He'd cleaned 'em all around in France,
No one in England stood a chance;
And I was champ in U. S. A.,
And knocked 'em cuckoo every day.

Now all McGee and me could think
Was how we'd like to cross the drink,
And knock this bucko for a row,
And grab a wagon load of dough.

At last Mac got me matched all right,
Five thousand smackers for the fight;
Then me and him packed up our grip,
And went to grab that championship.

I done some trainin' and the night
Set for the battle sure was right;
The crowd was wild, for this here bout
Was set to last till one was out.

The mob went crazy when the Pet
Came in, I'd never seen him yet;
And then I climbed up through the ropes,
All full of fight and full of hopes.

The crowd gave me an awful yell,
('Twas even money at the bell)
They stamped their feet and shook the place;
The Pet turned 'round, I saw his face!

My heart went sick, that's what it did,
For Holy Gee, it was the Kid!
We just had time for one good shake,
We meant it, too, it wasn't fake.

Whang! went the bell, the fight was on,
I clinched until the round was gone,
A-beggin', that he'd let me take
The fall for him—he wouldn't fake.

Heck, no, the Kid was on the square,
And said we had to fight it fair,
The crowd had bet their dough on us—
We had to fight (the honest cuss).

The referee was yellin' "break,"
The crowd was sore and howlin' "fake."
They'd paid their dough to see a scrap.
And so far we'd not hit a tap.

The second round we both begin.
I caught a fast one on my chin;
And stood like I was in a doze,
Until I got one on the nose.

I started landin' body blows,
He hooked another on my nose,
That riled my fightin' blood like hell,
And we was sluggin' at the bell.

The next round started, from the go
The millin' we did wasn't slow,
I landed hard on him, and then,
He took the count right up to ten.

He took the limit on one knee,
A chance to get his wind and see;
At nine he jumped up like a flash
And on my jaw he hung a smash.

I'm fightin', too, there, toe to toe,
And hittin' harder, blow for blow,
I sure soon knowed he couldn't stay,
He rolled his eyes—you know the way.

The way he staggered made me sick,
I stalled, McGee yelled "cop him quick!"
The crowd was wise and yellin' "fake,"
They'd seen the chance I wouldn't take.

The mob kept tellin' me to land,
And callin' things I couldn't stand;
I stepped in close and smashed his chin,
The Kid fell hard; he was all in.

I carried him into his chair,
And tried to bring him to for fair,
I rubbed his wrists, done everything,
A doctor climbed into the ring.

And I was scared as I could be,
The Kid was starin' and couldn't see;
The doctor turned and shook his head,
I looked again—the Kid was dead!

THIS old favorite is due for renewed popularity now that
television has brought the squared circle into thousands of
American homes. The difference between reading this poem
straight and reading it "in character" is the difference between
the diction award-winning announcer and the specialist in
sports announcing. The radio gravel voice of the Clem McCarthy is acceptable, and yes, loved by sports fans while horror
would be felt throughout the land if Clem were assigned to
announce the Philharmonic. The anonymous writer is no
Wordsworth, but he *is* a good story teller.

This is an illiterate poem, and properly so. It derives its
force by this very illiteracy. The fighter is simple minded; he
is not stupid, mind you, but he has a tongue whose muscles
have not been cultivated. The Kid has a hard time expressing
himself with his hands in his pockets. The poet has rhymed his
thoughts as a service to the Kid and an aid to the reader. But
beware of moving through this piece smoothly. The fighter has
a hard time telling his story. It doesn't come out in a straight
line; it spurts out.

The story is told in a minor key. Remember that the
fighter telling the story is not punch drunk. His trade gets into
a jamup with his emotions. He is sincere. He talks in jerks, but
not like one. Using a minor key effect and reading in phrases
will have a tendency to create a rolling monotony, but by
speeding up the action during the fight scenes you will break
up the sameness and at the same time set up the ending for
the proper elocutionary kayo.

This poem is not written completely in character; but must
be read that way. The fighter wouldn't say "this" or "them;"
it would sound more like "dis" and "em." Don't overdo the
dese, dems, and dose routine; it will make your audience lose
sympathy with the narrator. Strike a balance between Sands

Point and Jacobs Beach. Slur your words slightly. Speak your phrases in jabs rather than in roundhouse swings.

Realize, too, that the fighter is most descriptive where action is detailed. For example, in the second stanza with the words "give and take" make him feel the blow and the return wallop. In the fifth stanza, we have an inkling of the fighter's sensitivity when he tells how he used to dream of his friend. He states his frustration with the flat statement "he couldn't write."

The fighter drops his sadness in the sixth stanza. He is full of pride when he recites his record; he is boastful but in that tone that also seems to say, "Aw, gee, it wasn't nuthin'." In the tenth stanza he has forgotten about the Kid temporarily; he is excited with his own career. He builds up the tempo, the words come faster because he is on surer ground; he is talking about himself and describing *physical* sensations that he is more easily able to express. But the moment he runs up against an emotional problem, he experiences difficulty in describing it. In the fifteenth stanza, his fast pace stops dead in the last line right after the words. "The Pet turned round." Break off abruptly and read the words "I saw his face" as though the breath has suddenly been knocked out of you. It's only at the twentieth stanza that the fighter breaks his slow pace. He now moves as fast as his fists. Your reading parallels his physical effort. You breathe harder, clench your fingers and mould them into fists. Feel the effort of the blows as you read. When you reach the second stanza from the end, your breath is coming hard; start slowing down again.

The end of this poem is like the running down of a phonograph after the motor has been turned off; slow down gradually.

In making the record of this piece, the reader found it helpful to place his script on a stand and leave his hands and body free to follow the movements of the fighter. In the slow passages he stood flatfooted; when the action intensified he rose up on the balls of his feet. Try it.

A VISIT FROM ST. NICHOLAS

Clement C. Moore

'Twas the night before Christmas, when all through
　the house
Not a creature was stirring, not even a mouse;
The stockings were hung by the chimney with care,
In hopes that St. Nicholas soon would be there;
The children were nestled all snug in their beds,
While visions of sugar-plums danced in their heads;
And mamma in her kerchief, and I in my cap,
Had just settled our brains for a long winter's nap—
When out on the lawn there arose such a clatter,
I sprang from my bed to see what was the matter.
Away to the window I flew like a flash,
Tore open the shutters and threw up the sash.
The moon on the breast of the new-fallen snow
Gave a lustre of midday to objects below;
When, what to my wondering eyes should appear,
But a miniature sleigh and eight tiny reindeer,
With a little old driver, so lively and quick
I knew in a moment it must be St. Nick.
More rapid than eagles his coursers they came,
And he whistled and shouted, and called them by name:

"Now, Dasher! now, Dancer! now, Prancer and Vixen!
On, Comet! on, Cupid! on, Donder and Blitzen!
To the top of the porch, to the top of the wall!
Now dash away, dash away, dash away all!"
As dry leaves that before the wild hurricane fly,
When they meet with an obstacle, mount to the sky,
So up to the house-top the coursers they flew,
With the sleigh full of toys—and St. Nicholas too.
And then in a twinkling I heard on the roof
The prancing and pawing of each little hoof.
As I drew in my head, and was turning around,
Down the chimney St. Nicholas came with a bound.
He was dressed all in fur from his head to his foot,
And his clothes were all tarnished with ashes and soot;
A bundle of toys he had flung on his back,
And he looked like a pedler just opening his pack.
His eyes how they twinkled! his dimples how merry!
His cheeks were like roses, his nose like a cherry;
His droll little mouth was drawn up like a bow,
And the beard on his chin was as white as the snow.
The stump of a pipe he held tight in his teeth,
And the smoke it encircled his head like a wreath.
He had a broad face and a little round belly
That shook, when he laughed, like a bowl full of jelly.
He was chubby and plump—a right jolly old elf,

And I laughed, when I saw him, in spite of myself.

A wink of his eye and a twist of his head

Soon gave me to know I had nothing to dread.

He spoke not a word, but went straight to his work,

And filled all the stockings; then turned with a jerk,

And laying his finger aside of his nose,

And giving a nod, up the chimney he rose.

He sprang to his sleigh, to his team gave a whistle,

And away they all flew like the down of a thistle;

But I heard him exclaim, ere he drove out of sight,

"Happy Christmas to all, and to all a good-night!"

THIS is Santa Claus' calling card. The reading is an oraliza-
tion of the Santa Claus personality—warm, energetic, festive.
Too often has the start of this poem been kept in the *mysterioso*
key of Inner Sanctum. This effect is created by whispering the
opening lines as though the reader were afraid to be an
awakening alarm clock. In actuality, the poem is told from the
perspective of the father of the family who is wide awake
though he has just gone to bed. This is a poem with a smile.

The opening lines are a variation on the "Once Upon a
Time" technique of story telling. The opening phrase " 'Twas
the night before Christmas" parallels the fairy tale phrase. The
rest of the first line and all of the second are treated as a unit.
In the fifth and sixth lines lanolize your voice with the picture
of these cuddly children, bringing a smile to your face which
should be reflected in your voice. The ninth line calls for an
immediate acceleration of tempo as though you stepped on
the starter of your car and pushed the pedal way down to
get past another automobile. This and the four lines following
are read with a fast pace, suggesting real action. Now, as
quickly as you accelerated the pace, push down on the brake.
You are looking out on a beautiful scene and you must match
it with your voice quality and pace. In the eighteenth line,
bring into your voice the excitement of discovery. Underline
the word, "must."

When you reach Santa's speech, characterize the bearded
one in a manner of your own choosing; each person has a
different idea of the reindeer man. At the twenty-fifth line, by
dropping the Santa characterization, you will automatically
create a change of pace. A fast tempo should be used through
the thirtieth line.

At this point Santa comes in for a closeup. Your voice can be lowered, as you become more descriptive. In describing Santa, do it with good humor and understanding. You can, by your reading, set him up as a dirty old man or as a cute fellow who looks wonderful just because he's messed up.

As you approach the lines that refer to his eyes, dimples, cheeks and nose, don't run the descriptive words together. Read them as though you were seaching for just the exact word that is most apt. So we would have: "His eyes . . . how they twinkled"; "his dimples . . . how merry."

The fourth line from the end again calls for a change of pace. The clue to the reading lies in the word "sprang." The last line again recalls your characterization of Santa.

The challenge of this interpretation is in the creation of an interesting fabric of performance. This is not a poem made out of a solid color. It is a brightly colored pattern. You achieve this flavor and avoid a pastel performance by changing tone and pace at the suggested points.

THE VILLAGE BLACKSMITH

Henry Wadsworth Longfellow

Under a spreading chestnut-tree
The village smithy stands;
The smith, a mighty man is he,
With large and sinewy hands;
And the muscles of his brawny arms
Are strong as iron bands.

His hair is crisp, and black, and long,
His face is like the tan;
His brow is wet with honest sweat,
He earns whate'er he can,
And looks the whole world in the face,
For he owes not any man.

Week in, week out, from morn till night,
You can hear his bellows blow;
You can hear him swing his heavy sledge,
With measured beat and slow,
Like a sexton ringing the village bell,
When the evening sun is low.

And children coming home from school
Look in at the open door;
They love to see the flaming forge,
And hear the bellows roar,
And catch the burning sparks that fly
Like chaff from a threshing-floor.

He goes on Sunday to the church,
And sits among his boys;
He hears the parson pray and preach,
He hears his daughter's voice
Singing in the village choir,
And it makes his heart rejoice.

It sounds to him like her mother's voice,
Singing in Paradise!
He needs must think of her once more,
How in the grave she lies;
And with his hard, rough hand he wipes
A tear out of his eyes.

Toiling—rejoicing—sorrowing,
Onward through life he goes;
Each morning sees some task begin,
Each evening sees it close;
Something attempted, something done,
Has earned a night's repose.

Thanks, thanks to thee, my worthy friend,
For the lesson thou hast taught!
Thus at the flaming forge of life
Our fortunes must be wrought;
Thus on its sounding anvil shaped
Each burning deed and thought!

HAD Longfellow not been adept at rhyme and blessed instead, or in addition, with the facility of an artist, he would have been the best editorial page cartoonist of all times. True, all poets fill their works with rich imagery, and paint scenes with words and append morals. But Longfellow had that particular calico touch: he was a master of simple images— of basic moralizing. Longfellow has plenty of mass appeal. His symbolisms are readily understood.

The Village Blacksmith falls into this pattern. And here, despite the Chinese proverb, we have slightly under a thousand words that are as good as one picture. The first seven stanzas of this piece are the cartoon, the eighth is the caption.

The picture of the smithy is drawn with broad strokes. The reader will not *be* the smith, but, like all short men, he will stretch himself out in the presence of a husky visitor. Throw back your shoulders, flex your muscles, and in your reading describe the smith with a voice that is strong and muscular.

In the third line, pause after "smith," then follow up by underlining the word "mighty." In the fourth line emphasize "large" and "sinewy."

In the third stanza, the camera is swung away from the smith. Change your tone, slow down your pace. The fourth calls for a lighter, brighter note to follow the measured patterns of the preceding stanza.

In the fifth, a religious note is injected. This and the following stanza should be read in the manner of a respectful person who is talking to the person seated next to him during service on Sunday. It is almost, but not quite, whispered. It is softer in texture than the rest of the work. In the seventh stanza, start to build up again. This will be particularly effective if you follow the physical action described in the last two lines of the sixth stanza. Slow down and read these two lines in a halting style.

In the eighth stanza, return to the strength of the first. In the third line, emphasize "thus." In the fourth "our." In the fifth, again underline "thus" and "shaped." Pause before reading "shaped." It is a word that carries the heavy burden of describing the actual work involved in having a good life.

As if voice qualities were displayed in swatches like material, choose for the reading of the Village Blacksmith a rough, strong, tweedy sample. Rich resonances and smooth textures will not give this work its proper feel.

JENNY KISS'D ME
James Henry Leigh Hunt

Jenny kissed me when we met,
Jumping from the chair she sat in.
Time, you thief! who love to get
Sweets into your list, put that in.
Say I'm weary, say I'm sad;
Say that health and wealth have missed me;
Say I'm growing old, but add—
Jenny kissed me.

THIS is a poem with pinpoint carbonation; it sparkles like a glass of champagne. It bubbles over with good feeling. Here is an old man (think of C. Aubrey Smith of the movies) who is electrified by the kiss of a pretty young girl. He is excited, perhaps, not so much by the kiss itself as by the attention that was given him. Here is an older man announcing to the world, "There's still life in the old boy!" The annotator believes that Jenny is a young thing, maybe twelve or so, who has brightened up an old man's life with a youthful peck and given him something to write in on the credit side of his well-filled ledger.

The usual method of suggesting age by direct characterization is most easily accomplished by a slow and measured pace. But—the reverse should be used. Get the quality of age into your voice by characterization, but keep your pace at a brisk clip. Give some of that quality which is often referred to as "the joy of living."

In the third line raise your voice volume, speak directly to Time, who represents a constant opponent over whom you've just scored a triumph. Make it sound as though you're challenging him to do his worst, but you have found a new ally. Keep building this up until the line second to last when you will break off after "but add" and shift into a slower gear. The last line makes or breaks the poem. Read it as though someone had just given you a million dollars.

TO THE VIRGINS,
TO MAKE MUCH OF TIME
Robert Herrick

Gather ye rosebuds while ye may,
    Old Time is still a-flying:
And this same flower that smiles to-day
    Tomorrow will be dying.

The glorious lamp of heaven, the sun,
    The higher he's a-getting,
The sooner will his race be run,
    And nearer he's to setting.

That age is best which is the first,
    When youth and blood are warmer;
But being spent, the worse, and worst
    Times still succeed the former.

Then be not coy, but use your time,
    And while ye may, go marry:
For having lost but once your prime,
    You may for ever tarry.

HERRICK'S injunction to young ladies everywhere is a slice of advice offered with a smiling face and a warning finger. Doctors, lawyers, dentists and other professional men who sell their skill have loudly proclaimed that all they have to sell as a commodity is their time. Women sell their good looks, says Mr. Herrick, in accordance with time, too. And to refer to an age-honored proverb: procrastination is the thief of time. Mr. Herrick believes in early marriages. A witty lady pointed out that this is a moral poem; the last stanza carries the word "marry" and not "merry."

In reading this advice, please remember that it is not to be done in the style of the worried parent who is holding his daughter's dowry in one hand and warding off her man-less future in the other. Instead, this is the plea of a charming man seeking to help an indecisive woman make up her mind. That would make it one of the neatest tricks of the past few centuries.

Give this one a light reading. In the third stanza, use a warm manner and a softer voice. In the last stanza, by emphasizing the verbs, you will avoid the danger of a "remember, I warned you" tone. Underline "be," "use," "go." Remember, above all, that this poem derives its flavor not from scaring up the future, but by promising the pleasantness of the present.

FOR WHOM THE BELL TOLLS

John Donne

No man is an island,
    entire of *itself;*
Every man
    is a *piece* of the Continent,
    a *part* of the main.

If a Clod be *washed away* by the sea
    Europe is the less
As well
    as if a promontory were;
As well
    as if a manor of thy friend's
    or of thine own were.

Any man's death *diminishes* me,
    because I am involved in Mankind;
And therefore—
    Never *send* to know for whom the bell tolls:
It tolls for thee.

To HAVE offered the authentic version of this fragment from John Donne's *The Tolling Bell,* we would have had to print this piece in its original form in straight prose and with Old English spelling. ("Less" would have been spelled "lesse"; "entire," "intire".) This would have done a disservice to the poetic nature of the thought and built a barrier against this work in its logical application to contemporary problems. Therefore, the annotator has taken the liberty with this, as he has with several other works in this volume, of re-arranging the typographical presentation.

Here is a brilliant slogan that is both a weapon *against* isolationism and a preachment *for* the brotherhood of man. Too often have readers used this as a weapon without realizing the full scope of its application in the more positive sermonizing of greater understanding between men and nations.

This work derives its impact from a reading that carries a sureness and quiet conviction. Speak it as though it is undebatable; here is a fact, incontrovertible and unchallengable. It is from the measured sureness of your style that you will evoke the proper response. Read it quietly, deeply (both in voice and feeling). Pause often to let the words sink in. Since we have taken the liberty of re-arrangement, we have used this reader's license to italicize the words that require emphasis.

THE OWL AND THE PUSSY-CAT
Edward Lear

The Owl and the Pussy-cat went to sea
    In a beautiful pea-green boat:
They took some honey, and plenty of money
    Wrapped up in a five-pound note.
The Owl looked up to the stars above,
    And sang to a small guitar,
"O lovely Pussy, O Pussy, my love,
    What a beautiful Pussy you are,
            You are,
            You are!
What a beautiful Pussy you are!"

Pussy said to the Owl, "You elegant fowl,
    How charmingly sweet you sing!
Oh! let us be married; too long we have tarried:
    But what shall we do for a ring?"
They sailed away, for a year and a day,
    To the land where the bong-tree grows;
And there in a wood a Piggy-wig stood,
    With a ring at the end of his nose,
            His nose,
            His nose,
With a ring at the end of his nose.

"Dear Pig, are you willing to sell for one shilling
 Your ring?" Said the Piggy, "I will."
So they took it away, and were married next day
 By the Turkey who lives on the hill.
They dined on mince and slices of quince,
 Which they ate with a runcible spoon;
And hand in hand, on the edge of the sand,
 They danced by the light of the moon,
The moon,
The moon,
 They danced by the light of the moon.

EDWARD LEAR'S nonsense verse, is a poetic parallel of a Walt Disney technicolor short subject. In reading, an excellent effect is achieved by relating the piece in the manner of a Gilbert and Sullivan patter song. The words fall into a definite pattern and the rhyming scheme is easy and fluid. Follow the poet's meter.

Despite the nonsense quality of this work, the reader must be careful to avoid caricature. We are faced with the sometimes hairline distinction between a cartoon-character of the Disney type and a caricature-cartoon of the Peter Arno set. The owl and the pussycat are not prototypes; they're as real as Mickey Mouse and Donald Duck; they represent unique persons, rather than a lumped-up repository of people symbolizing a class or type.

There is a great deal of charm in this piece that can be easily distorted by overplaying. Keep your reading simple and moving at a fairly brisk pace. Don't attempt a characterization of the various speeches. While this is sometimes an effective device, in this particular case it will have a tendency to slow down the pace of your reading.

THE ARROW AND THE SONG
Henry Wadsworth Longfellow

I shot an arrow into the air,
It fell to earth, I knew not where;
For, so swiftly it flew, the sight
Could not follow it in its flight.

I breathed a song into the air,
It fell to earth, I knew not where;
For who has sight so keen and strong,
That it can follow the flight of song?

Long, long afterward, in an oak
I found the arrow, still unbroke;
And the song, from beginning to end,
I found again in the heart of a friend.

HERE is a study in parallels. In selecting the twin symbols of an arrow and a song, Longfellow gives direction and substance to what is usually conceived as an effervescent and disappearing act of the spirit. Here the song takes on the substances and the impact of the arrow. Structurally, the first two stanzas are husband and wife, and the third becomes their offspring. In reading it aloud, a pause after the second stanza (count three slowly) and a slower pace will give effective results. Simplicity in reading to match the simplicity of the symbols will give the most effective result. The question found in the last two lines of the second stanza should not be inflected too much; it is more rhetorical than demanding of an answer. In the third stanza, phrase your reading so that there is a flow of motion until after the three words "I found again . . ." in the last line. Pause here. Then in an even softer voice, and with great warmth read, "In the heart of a friend." If you draw a picture in your mind of a dear friend, you will hit this warm note with the proper elocutionary temperature.

OZYMANDIAS OF EGYPT

Percy Bysshe Shelley

I met a traveller from an antique land
Who said: Two vast and trunkless legs of stone
Stand in the desert . . . Near them, on the sand,
Half sunk, a shattered visage lies, whose frown,
And wrinkled lip, and sneer of cold command,
Tell that its sculptor well those passions read
Which yet survive, stamped on these lifeless things,
The hand that mocked them and the heart that fed:
And on the pedestal these words appear:
"My name is Ozymandias, king of kings:
Look on my works, ye Mighty, and despair!"
Nothing beside remains, Round the decay
Of that colossal wreck, boundless and bare,
The lone and level sands stretch far away.

HERE is a poem that deals with the twin and opposite emotions of hope and decay. Shelley uses his theme of decay on which to build a platform of hope. This poem reminds me of the last line in Maxwell Anderson's "High Tor," in which he says, "Nothing on earth is made by man, but makes in the end good ruins." Here is a lesson in living that isolates the act of acquiring possession from the act of acquiring immortality. The King, without a discerning crystal ball into the future, had engraved as his epitaph a line of advice for thoughtful people. Ozymandias intended to perpetuate himself in stone, and wound up preaching an unintended sermon to those who looked upon his monument. He had demonstrated but had not learned that stones are not immortal, either.

This is a thoughtful poem; to realize its possibilities you must correctly portray the hauteur and grandeur of the model of the statue. The editorial by Shelley starts in the third line from the end directly after the words, "Nothing beside remains." Pause a moment after this phrase and speak the moral slowly. The slower you read it, the more effective it will be. The bulk of the poem up to this moment should be read as though there were quotes around the words, beginning, "Two vast and" . . . and ending with . . . "nothing beside remains." The two and one half lines that round out the poem are the answer. This is a rewarding work. Its effectiveness depends on your understanding rather than on your vocal chords.

THE GLOVE AND THE LIONS

James Henry Leigh Hunt

King Francis was a hearty king, and loved a royal sport,
And one day, as his lions fought, sat looking on the
court.
The nobles filled the benches, with the ladies in their
pride,
And 'mongst them sat the Count de Lorge, with one
for whom he sighed:
And truly 'twas a gallant thing to see that crowning
show,
Valor and love, and a king above, and the royal beasts
below.

Ramped and roared the lions, with horrid laughing
jaws;
They bit, they glared, gave blows like beams, a wind
went with their paws;
With wallowing might and stifled roar they rolled on
one another,
Till all the pit with sand and mane was in a thunderous
smother;
The bloody foam above the bars came whisking through
the air;
Said Francis then, "Faith, gentlemen, we're better here
than there."

De Lorge's love o'erheard the King, a beauteous lively
    dame,
With smiling lips and sharp bright eyes, which always
    seemed the same;
She thought, "The Count my lover is brave as brave
    can be;
He surely would do wondrous things to show his love
    of me;
King, ladies, lovers, all look on; the occasion is divine;
I'll drop my glove, to prove his love; great glory will
    be mine."

She dropped her glove, to prove his love, then looked at
    him and smiled;
He bowed, and in a moment leaped among the lions
    wild:
The leap was quick, return was quick, he has regained
    his place,
Then threw the glove, but not with love, right in the
    lady's face.
"By Heaven," said Francis, "rightly done!" and he rose
    from where he sat;
"No love," quoth he, "but vanity, sets love a task like
    that."

THIS poem is a technicolor production in the grand style of Cecil B. DeMille. It has pageantry, excitement, crowd scenes, royalty of both two-legged and four-legged variety, suspense, gallantry, love interest. On this comparison we rest our case of advice. Study this poem, and treat it as though it were a movie. Use long shots, closeups, middle shots. Act it out as though it were a scenario.

We open with a panoramic shot, pausing to touch momentarily on the performers in our play, pan the camera at the end of the first stanza to a long shot of the lions in an arena. After the first line of the second stanza, we switch back to a closeup of King Francis. We then dissolve to train the camera on the Count and his lady love. Closeup on the lady as she thinks (starting on line three, stanza three). The sound track has her speaking. You hear her thoughts, but her lips don't move. Then . . . Action! The camera follows her hand as she drops her glove. The Count jumps in the arena, and the huge throng quiets down by the upraised hand of suspense. Then he acts . . . he throws the glove right in her face. There is an ominous silence. What will the king say! The camera shifts to him. He stands erect and speaks the curtain lines.

Red-flag the temptation to be shouty . . . excitement and suspense achieve their greatest effects by intensity rather than by volume. Characterize the King when he speaks, the lovely lady when she thinks aloud. Characterize the lions in stanza two; it's important to set up the danger inherent in the lady's challenge. Such phrases as "Blows like beams," "They glared, they bit," all should be acted out. Being a lion is the most difficult kind of type-casting, but to create the proper canvas of savagery, you will have to make those lions vivid.

Note particularly, Hunt's use of double rhymes. These are signals for handling of the phrases, for the rhyme inside of an outside rhyme calls for a pause when it appears. You'll find samples of this in the second line where "fought" completes a thought even before the rhyming "court" appears. The last line of the first stanza demonstrates another such point. "Valor and love, and a king above," are a rhyme within a rhyme. Another important use is in the very last line of the poem, "No love," quoth he, "but Vanity." Here again the "vanity" rhyming with the "quoth he" calls for a short pause. You'll see that this ingenious device permits you to give proper emphasis to the important words that follow. Pauses are as effective in framing a phrase as reading one set of words louder than the other.

BREAK, BREAK, BREAK

Alfred, Lord Tennyson

Break, break, break,
On thy cold gray stones, O Sea!
And I would that my tongue could utter
The thoughts that arise in me.

O, well for the fisherman's boy,
That he shouts with his sister at play!
O, well for the sailor lad,
That he sings in his boat on the bay!

And the stately ships go on
To the haven under the hill;
But O for the touch of a vanish'd hand,
And the sound of a voice that is still!

Break, break, break,
At the foot of thy crags, O Sea!
But the tender grace of a day that is dead
Will never come back to me.

IN a mythical newspaper an anonymous writer inserted into a non-existent want-ad column the following, "Lost: Yesterday. Two precious hours. No reward is offered because they are gone forever."

Tennyson says the same thing in this little vignette full of sound and sadness. He counterpoints his loss against the constant sway of the ocean. The interpretive challenge is to keep a lump in your throat without getting a break in your voice.

The measured rhythm of the titled words is a lure to carry this rhythm constantly through the reading. Yet the effectiveness of the interpretation depends on your ability to break the rhythm and personalize the grief. As indicated in other analysis in this volume, many readers treat the emotions in the poems as observers rather than as participants. They tell about the poet's problems without sharing them. Poetry is an emotional experience and the full realization of the emotional pattern is checkmated unless the interpreter "lives the part." This does not mean that a reading of a poem in which the writer goes mad calls for the reader to follow him into an asylum. Rather it suggests a fashion of sympathetic vibration, allowing you to control the situation, interpret it through understanding, and then move away from it. The fine interpreter is like a radio set; he manipulates the bass and treble knobs, the volume control, and knows when to turn the machine on and off. Yet, throughout he tunes in to the wave-length on which the original author is broadcasting. The reader is his own Federal Communications Commission and must allocate the channels of emotion; it is this ability that differentiates the ham from the Hamlet.

HOW DO I LOVE THEE?

Elizabeth Barrett Browning

How do I love thee? Let me count the ways.
I love thee to the depth and breadth and height
My soul can reach, when feeling out of sight
For the ends of Being and ideal Grace.
I love thee to the level of every day's
Most quiet need, by sun and candle-light.
I love thee freely, as men strive for Right;
I love thee purely, as men turn from Praise.
I love thee with the passion put to use
In my old griefs, and with my childhood's faith.
I love thee with a love I seemed to lose
With my lost saints,—I love thee with the breath,
Smiles, tears, of all my life!—and, if God choose,
I shall but love thee better after death.

(*from* SONNETS FROM THE PORTUGUESE)

THE secret to the proper vocal interpretation of this sonnet rests in the first line. This line is a stanza by itself—it is the theme that must be stated clearly. What follows is the embellishment. If the proper reading of the theme is lost, the sonnet goes by default. Perhaps this will help you most: Before reading the first line, imagine someone asking you, someone you love, "How do you love me?" That's a hard question to answer and you think about the best way to answer, almost musing to yourself, *"How* do I love thee? Let me *count the ways."* The italicized words are those to be stressed. Obviously here is a problem; you love this person in so *many* ways that a simple answer won't cover your response. What follows is a sort of amatory bookkeeping. Don't pyramid each point, rather treat each reason separately. In handling the last line, remember that you are switching from the first person singular to the Most Singular Person. Treat this line differently, reverently. Pause after the word "better" in the last line and tie the sonnet up neatly by a simple and sincere reading of the words ". . . after death."

PAUL REVERE'S RIDE

Henry Wadsworth Longfellow

Listen, my children, and you shall hear
Of the midnight ride of Paul Revere,
On the eighteenth of April, in Seventy-Five:
Hardly a man is now alive
Who remembers that famous day and year.

He said to his friend, "If the British march
By land or sea from the town to-night,
Hang a lantern aloft in the belfry arch
Of the North Church tower as a signal-light,
One, if by land, and two, if by sea;
And I on the opposite shore will be,
Ready to ride and spread the alarm
Through every Middlesex village and farm,
For the country folk to be up to arm.

Then he said, Good night! and with muffled oar
Silently rowed to the Charlestown shore,
Just as the moon rose over the bay,
Where swinging wide at her moorings lay
The Somerset, British man-of-war;
A phantom ship, with each mast and spar
Across the moon like a prison bar,
And a huge black hulk, that was magnified
By its own reflection in the tide.

Meanwhile, his friend, through alley and street
Wanders and watches with eager ears,
Till in the silence around him he hears
The muster of men at the barrack door,
The sound of arms, and the tramp of feet,
And the measured tread of the grenadiers,
Marching down to their boats on the shore.
Then he climbed to the tower of the Old North Church,
By the wooden stairs, with stealthy tread,
To the belfry-chamber overhead,
And startled the pigeons from their perch
On the sombre rafters, that round him made
Masses and moving shapes of shade,—
By the trembling ladder, steep and tall,
To the highest window in the wall,
Where he paused to listen and look down
A moment on the roofs of the town,
And the moonlight flowing over all.

Beneath, in the churchyard, lay the dead,
In their night-encampment on the hill,
Wrapped in silence so deep and still
That he could hear, like a sentinel's tread,
The watchful night-wind, as it went
Creeping along from tent to tent,

And seeming to whisper, "All is well!"
A moment only he feels the spell
Of the place and the hour, and the secret dread
Of the lonely belfry and the dead;
For suddenly all his thoughts are bent
On a shadowy something far away,
Where the river widens to meet the bay,—
A line of black that bends and floats
On the rising tide, like a bridge of boats.

Meanwhile, impatient to mount and ride,
Booted and spurred, with a heavy stride
On the opposite shore walked Paul Revere.
Now he patted his horse's side,
Now gazed at the landscape far and near,
Then, impetuous, stamped the earth,
And turned and tightened his saddle-girth:
But mostly he watched with eager search
The belfry-tower of the Old North Church,
As it rose above the graves on the hill,
Lonely, and spectral, and sombre and still.
And lo! as he looks, on the belfry's height
A glimmer, and then a beam of light!
He springs to the saddle, the bridle he turns
But lingers and gazes, till full on his sight

A second lamp in the belfry burns!
A hurry of hoofs in a village street,
A shape in the moonlight, a bulk in the dark,
And beneath, from the pebbles, in passing, a spark
Struck out by a steed flying fearless and fleet:
That was all! And yet, through the gloom and the light,
The fate of a nation was riding that night;
And the spark struck out by that steed, in his flight,
Kindled the land into flame with its heat.

He has left the village and mounted the steep,
And beneath him, tranquil and broad and deep,
Is the Mystic, meeting the ocean tides;
And under the alders, that skirt its edge,
Now soft on the sand, now loud on the ledge,
Is heard the tramp of his steed as he rides.

It was twelve by the village clock
When he crossed the bridge into Medford town
He heard the crowing of the cock,
And the barking of the farmer's dog,
And felt the damp of the river fog.

It was one by the village clock,
When he rode into Lexington.

He saw the gilded weathercock
Swim in the moonlight as he passed,
And the meeting-house windows, blank and bare,
Gaze at him with a spectral glare,
As if they already stood aghast
At the bloody work they would look upon.

It was two by the village clock,
When he came to the bridge in Concord town.
He heard the bleating of the flock,
And the twitter of birds among the trees,
And felt the breath of the morning breeze
Blowing over the meadows brown.
And one was safe and asleep in his bed
Who at the bridge would be first to fall,
Who that day would be lying dead,
Pierced by a British musket-ball.
You know the rest. In the books you have read,
How the British Regulars fired and fled,—
How the farmers gave them ball for ball,
From behind each fence and farm-yard wall,
Chasing the red-coats down the lane,
Then crossing the fields to emerge again
Under the trees at the turn of the road,
And only pausing to fire and load.

So through the night rode Paul Revere;

And so through the night went his cry of alarm

To every Middlesex village and farm,—

A cry of defiance and not of fear,

A voice in the darkness, a knock at the door,

And a word that shall echo forevermore!

For, borne on the night-wind of the Past,

Through all our history, to the last,

In the hour of darkness and peril and need,

The people will waken and listen to hear

The hurrying hoof-beats of that steed,

And the midnight message of Paul Revere.

HERE is an American Classic, a statue carved out of words. One of the most familiar of American poems, it is a skillful combination of picture painting and horse opera. Because of the length of this work, careful blending of the ingredients are suggested. Here is a challenge to the reader, not so much of pace, but of change of pace. In order to keep up the interest you will tire yourself and your auditors unless you bring a great deal of variety to your interpretation. This is best accomplished by shrewd changes of tempo. The clues that Longfellow gives are most helpful, particularly when you watch for the rhyming patterns, which are not the same throughout the poem. Thus, Longfellow himself suggests the places for the changes of tempo. This also helps form the breathing patterns for the reader. Breaths are never taken between sentences except where the sentence completes a thought. You will find that a comma makes a good resting post, providing the thought-pattern allows for it. The poem starts off in the grand manner for the first stanza. Then we find Revere setting the plot. Stanza three is description; you can slow up on this one. Following is a stanza of plot development, the action is about to begin, the carpet of suspense is being laid down—you walk quietly over it. There are some nice Alfred Hitchcock touches—the pigeons that flutter, "the moving shapes of shade," the trembling ladder and "the moonlight flowing over all." Then a pastoral note is sounded, pure and descriptive. Stanza seven calls for a change of pace, the action accelerates. Count thirteen lines down in this stanza and mark it as the place to really move along with your fastest tempo. It is at this point that all the quietness of the earlier stanzas is left behind. Here the change of pace is from fast to very fast. Six lines from the end of the poem, take a pause after the "For" and switch your reading to accommodate the moral. For here Longfellow suggests, and you must communicate this to your audience, that the "Ride of Paul Revere" was not only an historical fact but an American tradition—that in times of stress there must always be Paul Reveres to wake up the country; that people need a symbolic man on horseback who will call them to arms to fight off the enemy, whether he wear a red coat or a white sheet.

SONNET 29

William Shakespeare

When in disgrace with fortune and men's eyes
I all alone beweep my outcast state,
And trouble deaf heaven with my bootless cries,
And look upon myself and curse my fate,
Wishing me like to one more rich in hope,
Featured like him, like him with friends possessed,
Desiring this man's art, and that man's scope,
With what I most enjoy contented least;
Yet in these thoughts myself almost despising,
Haply I think on thee—and then my state,
Like to the lark at break of day arising
From sullen earth, sings hymns at heaven's gate;
    For thy sweet love remembered, such wealth brings
    That then I scorn to change my state with kings.

THE reading of Shakespeare's sonnets is facilitated by an understanding of the bard's years of service as playwright and actor. The proper stage direction and punctuation have been the guide sheets that a playwright interposes beween his work and his interpreters.

Poets without this theatre experience have not had the opportunities of interpretation and simply satisfy themselves. Shakespeare wrote his sonnets like his plays—to be read aloud. To insure their proper reading, he punctuates his words by thoughts, thus giving a clear road map to the reader.

Take this twenty-ninth sonnet. If written out in a prose style, you will note that it is one sentence—one of the longest sentences you ever came across.

The reading problems are basically those of breathing. Mr. Shakespeare calls for a lot of words in between breaths. Check the commas for the breathing spots. The first eight lines are to be pyramided. The poet is building up a bubble which he plans to burst in the last part of his sonnet. At the ninth line, there is a change cued by the semi-colon. Here the tortured mind is soothed by the gentle hand of love. Take a pause after the semi-colon, hold it a beat, and then continue in a softer tone.

FATHER WILLIAM

Lewis Carroll

"You are old, Father William," the young man said,
   "And your hair has become very white;
And yet you incessantly stand on your head—
   Do you think, at your age, it is right?"

"In my youth," Father William replied to his son,
   "I feared it might injure the brain;
But, now that I'm perfectly sure I have none,
   Why, I do it again and again."

"You are old," said the youth, "as I mentioned before,
   And have grown most uncommonly fat;
Yet you turned a back-somersault in at the door—
   Pray, what is the reason of that?"

"In my youth," said the sage, as he shook his gray locks,
   "I kept all my limbs very supple
By the use of this ointment—one shilling the box—
   Allow me to sell you a couple?"

"You are old," said the youth, "and your jaws are too
    weak
  For anything tougher than suet;
Yet you finished the goose, with the bones and the
    beak—
  Pray, how did you manage to do it?"

"In my youth," said his father, "I took to the law,
  And argued each case with my wife;
And the muscular strength which it gave to my jaw
  Has lasted the rest of my life."

"You are old," said the youth, "one would hardly
    suppose
  That your eye was as steady as ever;
Yet you balanced an eel on the end of your nose—
  What made you so awfully clever?"

"I have answered three questions, and that is enough,"
  Said his father. "Don't give yourself airs!
Do you think I can listen all day to such stuff?
  Be off, or I'll kick you down-stairs!"

LEWIS CARROLL, whose fame has increased in geometric progression, which is only proper for a teacher of mathematics, wrote this poem as a satire on a piece of Robert Southey. While the original is buried by the dust of a century, the satire has become one of the most renowned "nonsense" poems of the English language. Actually, the "old man" in the poem has an amazing streak of logic, and any father who has coped with the quiz-kid mind of an offspring will admire his patience through seven stanzas and appreciate his blow up in the last.

By reading the young man's lines with a faster pace than those of the father, and giving a quality of age to the old man's lines by slowing the pace down, and using a more deliberate style, you get a necessary contrast.

At the eighth stanza the father, who has fulfilled the old adage, "ask a silly question and you'll get a silly answer," reaches the breaking point. Slowly he builds up to an explosion. In the last two lines he explodes.

GENERAL JOHN

W. S. Gilbert

The bravest names for fire and flames
    And all that mortal durst,
Were GENERAL JOHN and PRIVATE JAMES,
    Of the Sixty-seventy-first.

GENERAL JOHN was a soldier tried,
    A chief of warlike dons;
A haughty stride and a withering pride
    Were MAJOR-GENERAL JOHN'S.

A sneer would play on his martial phiz,
    Superior birth to show;
"Pish!" was a favourite word of his,
    And he often said "Ho! ho!"

FULL-PRIVATE JAMES described might be,
    As a man of a mournful mind;
No characteristic trait had he
    Of any distinctive kind.

From the ranks, one day, cried PRIVATE JAMES,
    "Oh! MAJOR-GENERAL JOHN,
I've doubts of our respective names,
    My mournful mind upon.

"A glimmering thought occurs to me
  (Its source I can't unearth),
But I've a kind of a notion we
  Were cruelly changed at birth.

"I've a strange idea that each other's names
  We've each of us got on.
Such things have been," said PRIVATE JAMES.
  "They have!" sneered GENERAL JOHN.

"My GENERAL JOHN, I swear upon
  My oath I think 'tis so—"
"Pish!" proudly sneered his GENERAL JOHN,
  And he also said "Ho! ho!"

"My GENERAL JOHN! my GENERAL JOHN!
  My GENERAL JOHN!" quoth he,
"This aristocratical sneer upon
  Your face I blush to see!

"No truly great or generous cove
   Deserving of them names,
Would sneer at a fixed idea that's drove
   In the mind of a PRIVATE JAMES!"

Said GENERAL JOHN, "Upon your claims
   No need your breath to waste;
If this is a joke, FULL-PRIVATE JAMES,
   It's a joke of doubtful taste.

"But, being a man of doubtless worth,
   If you feel certain quite
That we were probably changed at birth,
   I'll venture to say you're right."

So GENERAL JOHN as PRIVATE JAMES
   Fell in, parade upon;
And PRIVATE JAMES, by change of names,
   Was MAJOR-GENERAL JOHN.

IF W. S. Gilbert were alive today it would be easy to peg his activities. He would certainly have a permanent spot on *Information Please* where he would mix the acid of Oscar Levant with the savoyardian knowledge of F. P. A. He would contribute a yearly score to Broadway's music halls, but above all, he would be a frequent contributor to *New Yorker* magazine. As a cartoonist (which he was) with pen and India ink, Gilbert is unexcelled. The key to the reading of this or any of his Bab Ballads is that his people are cartoons.

A cartoonist draws his characters, or should we say caricatures, with broad strokes. They are serious and from their seriousness is generated their laughability. Both General John and Private James help caricature the old army game. As GI's (Gilbert issues) they satirize the power and glory of the army in a "general" way. It is Mr. Gilbert's neat thesis that many a private could do as well as many a general, but for accident of birth rather than by quality of worth. In his poem, they change places without the customary red tape. Read this poem with a straight face. If an English accent is in your brogue's gallery, use it; but just a pinch of accent, please. The rhyming words should be overaccentuated. While this is not recommended procedure with serious poems, it is necessary to develop the proper cartoony quality. Another point to remember in reading this poem aloud is that here, unlike most of the others in this volume, the paragraphs do not run into each other. They are, in the parlance of photography, stills.

Before you go through the poem, mark up the rhyming words. In the first stanza, underline "flames" and "James," "durst" and "first." Lean on them in your preliminary reading. Follow suit in the subsequent stanzas. This emphasis on the rhymes will bring out the cartoon-like quality of the protagonists and will enable you to treat the rest of the poem seriously. Thus, the comic values are brought into focus without the blur of the typical "ham" reading.

DANNY DEEVER

Rudyard Kipling

"What are the bugles blowin' for?" said
    Files-on-Parade.
" To turn you out, to turn you out," the Colour-
    Sergeant said.
"What makes you look so white, so white?"
    said Files-on-Parade.
"I'm dreadin' what I've got to watch," the
    Colour-Sergeant said.

For they're hangin' Danny Deever, you
    can 'ear the Dead March play,
The regiment's in 'ollow square—they're
    hangin' him to-day;
They've taken of his buttons off an' cut
    his stripes away,
An' they're hangin' Danny Deever in the
    mornin'.

"What makes the rear-rank breathe so'ard?"
    said Files-on-Parade.
"It's bitter cold, it's bitter cold," the Colour-
    Sergeant said.
"What makes that front-rank man fall down?"
    said Files-on-Parade.
"A touch o' sun, a touch o' sun," the Colour-
    Sergeant said.

They are hangin' Danny Deever, they are
    marchin' of 'im round,
They 'ave 'alted Danny Deever by 'is coffin
    on the ground;
An ' 'e'll swing in 'arf a minute for a
    sneakin', shootin' hound—
O they're hangin' Danny Deever in the
    mornin'!

" 'Is cot was right-'and cot to mine,"said
    Files-on-Parade.
" 'E's sleepin' out an' far to-night," the Colour-
    Sergeant said.
"I've drunk' is beer a score o' times," said
    Files-on-Parade.
" 'E's drinkin' bitter beer alone," the Colour-
    Sergeant said.

They are hangin' Danny Deever, you must
    mark 'im to 'is place,
For'e shot a comrade sleepin'—you must
    look 'im in the face;
Nine 'undred of 'is county an' the
    regiment's disgrace,
While they're hangin' Danny Deever in
    the mornin'.

"What's that so black agin the sun?" said
    Files-on-Parade.
"It's Danny fightin' 'ard for life," the Colour-
    Sergeant said.
"What's that that whimpers over'ead?" said
    Files-on-Parade.
"It's Danny's soul that's passin' now," the
    Colour-Sergeant said.

For they're done with Danny Deever, you
    can 'ere the quickstep play,
The regiment's in column, an' they're
    marchin' us away;
Ho! the young recruits are shakin', an'
    they'll want their beer to-day,
After hangin' Danny Deever in the
    mornin'.

THE interpretive challenge of this poem is one of perspective. When we worked over this piece for recording, the component parts never seemed to fall into place to create a unified whole. When we realized that the flaw lay in the determination of the position of the two speakers in relation to the full-dress parade, and followed our belief, all the ragged edges smoothed out.

This is a horror poem. Don't be misled by the pageantry of the bright, full-dress uniforms in which England decks out its overseas armies. This is a funeral march, not a parade.

This poem is broken down into two units—each in alternating stanzas. Files-on-Parade and the Colour-Sergeant are two frightened people. They are standing at attention and the words they speak are under-the-breath remarks. They are staccato and nervous sentiments. Files-on-Parade is obviously young, inexperienced. His sergeant is an old hand and like any leader, tries to cheer-up one of his men. Obviously, the men who are witnessing the execution of Danny Deever have been brought there to sample the punishment that accrues to the evil-doer. Picture these men who have the choice of hypnotic watching or a weak-kneed I-can't-look-at-this attitude. The young soldier cannot focus on the hanging, and he keeps asking for information. The sergeant, rather than give a blow by blow account, finds excuses for everything. When Files-on-Parade asks him why the rear ranks breathe so hard, he answers, "It's bitter cold." He alibis fear with the climate.

When reading this poem aloud, treat the speeches of both men as underbreaths. Both are jittery and fear runs through their lines. The alternate stanzas are like drum beats—steady, repeated rhythm. It is with this device that Kipling generates the horror of the scene. In a way, it parallels the constant steady drum beats in the O'Neill play, *The Emperor Jones*. It is by bringing this motive back after each sequence between the two soldiers that the inevitability of the tragedy builds up its climax. For here is a climax that is built by equal emphasis rather than by any mounting volume.

If in reading "Danny Deever" you have the opportunity for music, we suggest that it be used only under the drum-roll passages, while leaving the conversation stanzas free of background.

If you have a facility for dialect, you can characterize the speeches. But care should be taken not to overdo it; bright colors would ruin this reading. It is a poem of greys.

WHEN I AM DEAD, MY DEAREST
Christina Rosetti

When I am dead, my dearest,
Sing no sad songs for me;
Plant thou no roses at my head,
Nor shady cypress-tree:
Be the green grass above me
With showers and dewdrops wet;
And if thou wilt, remember,
And if thou wilt, forget.

I shall not see the shadows,
I shall not feel the rain;
I shall not hear the nightingale
Sing on, as if in pain:
And dreaming through the twilight
That doth not rise nor set,
Haply I may remember,
And haply may forget.

REMEMBER ME WHEN I AM GONE AWAY

Christina Rosetti

Remember me when I am gone away,
Gone far away into the silent land;
When you can no more hold me by the hand,
Nor I half turn to go, yet turning stay.
Remember me when no more, day by day,
You tell me of our future that you planned:
Only remember me; you understand
It will be late to counsel then or pray.
Yet if you should forget me for a while
And afterwards remember, do not grieve:
For if the darkness and corruption leave
A vestige of the thoughts that once I had,
Better by far you should forget and smile
Than that you should remember and be sad.

CHRISTINA ROSETTI said, "I cannot possibly use the word 'happy' without meaning something beyond this present life." Small wonder, then, that her poems should deal with the hereafter. The great wonder, however, is in the sharp definition she gives to the afterworld. It's a very real place to her; her poems are tickets purchased for the train trip.

Despite the sweetness and gentle quality which is in these poems, there also is an iron fist inside the velvet glove. Death, says Miss Rossetti, leaves behind the remaining presence of the deceased. The moving finger may write, and having writ move on, but the presence of a deceased person always remains to haunt the companion who shared his life.

Reading these poems is an exercise in simplicity. Read them quietly. There is an element of pleading inherent in these works. In reading "When I am dead," pause after the first four words and speak the "my dearest" to somebody. In the seventh and eighth lines of the second stanzas the pause comes before "may remember" and "may forget." This is where the threat comes, so emphasize the two "mays."

"Remember Me" is of the genre. The key word in this poem is "remember." It is used five times, each for a specific effect. Here again what seemingly is a humble sadness is really a gentle threat; the poetess intends to stay with those who shared her breathing moments. Her weapon here is their memory. But being a gentle soul she tells them about it with her sad sweetness. In the first line, emphasize "me" slightly. This will force you to create a natural pause and enable you to build the second line on top of the last half of the first. In the fourth line again a slight emphasis on "half." The first phrase in the seventh line, "only remember me," belongs to the preceding line despite the punctuation. "You understand" starts a new forward motion of the poem. In the tenth lines emphasize the syllable "after" in "afterwards" and in the twelfth line, lean lightly on the word "vestige."

MY HEART LEAPS UP WHEN I BEHOLD
William Wordsworth

My heart leaps up when I behold
        A rainbow in the sky:
So was it when my life began;
So is it now I am a man;
So be it when I shall grow old,
        Or let me die!
The Child is father of the Man;
And I could wish my days to be
Bound each to each by natural piety

THIS simple and small slice of Wordsworth is a typical affirmation of the faith the poet had in nature, and his ability to get excited by simple and everyday beauties. Wordsworth doesn't "see" a rainbow in the sky, he "beholds" it; a word connoting much more action. His heart doesn't get "warm"— it "leaps up" when he sees a rainbow. Underline the words "leaps up" and accent them. The emphasis will result in a natural pause and an easy follow-through. In the fifth line, underline "be." The third, fourth, and fifth lines should be negotiated on one breath. This will call for a breathing spot and a simple reading of "Or let me die." The seventh line is a brilliant epigram and should be read to allow its import to be understood and confirmed by the closing words of the poem.

O CAPTAIN! MY CAPTAIN!
(Abraham Lincoln assassinated, April 15, 1865)

Walt Whitman

O Captain! my Captain, our fearful trip is done,

The ship has weather'd every rack, the prize we sought
is won,

The port is near, the bells I hear, the people all
exulting,

While follow eyes the steady keel, the vessel grim and
daring;

But O heart! heart! heart!

O the bleeding drops of red,

Where on the deck my Captain lies,

Fallen cold and dead.

O Captain! my Captain! rise up and hear the bells;

Rise up—for you the flag is flung—for you the bugle
trills,

For you bouquets and ribbon'd wreaths—for you the
shores a-crowding,

For you they call, the swaying mass, their eager faces
turning;

Here Captain! dear father!

The arm beneath your head!

It is some dream that on the deck,

You've fallen cold and dead.

My Captain does not answer, his lips are pale and still,

My father does not feel my arm, he has no pulse nor
will,

The ship is anchor'd safe and sound, its voyage closed
and done,

From fearful trip the victor ship comes in with object
won:

    Exult O shores, and ring O bells!

    But I with mournful tread,

      Walk the deck my Captain lies,

      Fallen cold and dead.

ABRAHAM LINCOLN today is as much an adjective as a proper name. Having witnessed the truncation of this piece by many willing but unknowing elocutionists, we have been inclined to index this poem as appropriate to a wailing wall rather than a poetic measure of the dignity and simplicity of the Lincoln Memorial in Washington. Yet, strangely enough, the variance between the most moving rendition of this piece and the cellar of interpretations lies in one word.

The sorrow inherent in this poem results directly from the personalization of the grief. Too often readers are wont to lump the first four words together. However, the emphasis of the word "my" preceding the second "captain" is the link between the reader and the dead President. Take this poem apart in your mind before you put it together with your tongue. "O Captain," and "My Captain" cannot be read in the same way. The first refers to Lincoln, the President; the second to Lincoln, the father. Pause after "O Captain," and then emphasize the word "my" and read the phrase in a softer tone than the values you give to "O Captain."

The strength of the poem consists largely of this emphasis. Another dash of distinction is the dramatic setting of the fallen captain and the welcoming throng. The people exult because the war between the States has ended, the occasion is worth the festival. But the personal loss of one of the warriors who brought victory and peace cannot be carried away and cancelled out by the welcome to peace.

In the third line, emphasize the words "port," "bells," "the people;" these represent the perspective of the celebrating crowd. The personalization (and these lines must be read slowl and more quietly than the first four) is in the closing lines of each stanza.

In the second stanza, underline the word "you" each of the five times it appears. The highest point of vocalization occurs in this stanza. Step up your pace in reading the first four lines. Then quietly kneel down and put your arm under his head. In the last stanza, bitterness is merged with the grief as the poet betrays the celebrants who have lost sight of their great leader in the excitement of victory.

In the last three lines, suit the action to the words. The pace is slow; it is mournful; it is measured. Treat each word as a step in a funeral march. Fallen . . . cold . . . and dead . . .

THE TYGER
William Blake

Tyger! Tyger! burning bright
In the forests of the night,
What immortal hand or eye
Could frame thy fearful symmetry?

In what distant deeps or skies
Burnt the fire of thine eyes?
On what wings dare he aspire?
What the hand dare seize the fire?

And what shoulder, and what art,
Could twist the sinews of thy heart?
And when thy heart began to beat,
What dread hand? and what dread feet?

What the hammer? what the chain?
In what furnace was thy brain?
What the anvil? what dread grasp
Dare its deadly terrors clasp?

When the stars threw down their spears
And watered heaven with their tears,
Did he smile his work to see?
Did he who made the Lamb make thee?

Tyger! Tyger! burning bright
In the forests of the night,
What immortal hand or eye
Dare frame thy fearful symmetry?

IN a recent motion picture, *Body and Soul,* the heroine in admiration of the physique of the champion prizefighter quotes the first four lines to him. Like so many who have read this poem he called for an explanation. Her choice of this poem to express the raw physical and animal-like strength of the prizefighter was strikingly appropriate.

As one of the *Songs of Experience,* this poem has been labeled as the symbolism of the Tyger (Experience) and the lamb (Innocence). Yet in reading this poem aloud, one increasingly realizes that the tiger represents the sensual and the lamb, the sensuous. One must remember that Blake was a genius in twin arts: painting and poetry. In any event, one is helped by conceding that his poems are pictures. The motion picture that incorporates the reference to this piece is a good clue to understanding, for perhaps the Tyger represents "the Body" and the lamb, "the Soul."

Here is a piece full of question marks, both in punctuation and interpretation. This is a deeply religious work. Perhaps it is more the work of an evangelist than a minister; the rich imagery of the poem is a sermon on the greatness of creation.

Try the first stanza. Instead of running the words together, treat them as pulse beats: Tyger (pause) Tyger (pause) Burning (pause) bright (pause) In (pause) the forests (pause) of (pause) the night (pause). If one treats the tyger as the embodiment of the physical, a powerful force is created that sweeps the entire poem. Stanzas two to five do not utilize this pulse beat rhythm, but the closing verse is a repetition of the first.

The first and last stanzas are identical with the exception
of one word in their last lines. In the repeat, the word "could"
is replaced by the word "dare." It is the opinion of the
annotator that the word dare is not used in its challenging
sense, but rather as an adjective of admiration.

We propose that the question marks serve the function
of exclamation points; the words "immortal hand or eye"
should be capped like other references to the Deity. Remember,
please, that Blake, while perhaps not religious in the formal
manner, is reported to have had visions all his life; it is said
that he saw God put his forehead against his window pane.
It is an admitted fact that attempted explanations of Blake's
intentions have all been varied and contradictory. This explanation is a background against which we draw in order to
validate our interpretation that denies the original punctuation
marks of the author.

In any event, as stated in the introduction to this volume,
perhaps this interpretation can serve as a punching bag for
your own theories and result in greater exploration and understanding.

THE DAFFODILS

William Wordsworth

I wandered lonely as a cloud
That floats on high o'er vales and hills,
When all at once I saw a crowd,
A host of golden daffodils,
Beside the lake, beneath the trees
Fluttering and dancing in the breeze.

Continuous as the stars that shine
And twinkle on the milky way,
They stretched in never-ending line
Along the margin of a bay:
Ten thousand saw I at a glance
Tossing their heads in sprightly dance.

The waves beside them danced, but they
Out-did the sparkling waves in glee:
A poet could not but be gay
In such a jocund company!
I gazed—and gazed—but little thought
What wealth the show to me had brought:

For oft, when on my couch I lie
In vacant or in pensive mood,
They flash upon that inward eye
Which is the bliss of solitude;
And then my heart with pleasure fills,
And dances with the daffodils.

THE tendency in reading this poem is to treat it as a pastel vignette. Despite the pastoral quality of the description, one must bring to the reading of this work the energy of discovery. In the last portion of the poem, Wordsworth admits that he had not properly pegged the value of the scene. The snare rests in the first line: one is apt to be as lazy as a floating cloud. So, ease into this poem for the opening two lines, but then generate the excitement of discovery as the scene shakes the poet from his lassitude. A neat way to do this is to treat the word "host" as a development of the word "crowd" in the preceding line. This is not a picture taken by a still camera, but a motion picture. Give life to "fluttering and dancing," "tossing their heads in sprightly dance." This is no inanimate scene, and one must respond with an animated reading. After the opening lines, with the exception of the meditative conclusion of the last stanza, give this a brisk reading. The last verse is a follow-up to the entire poem. Note the semi-colon that leads into it. Lean on the word "dances" in the last line of the work.

CASEY AT THE BAT

Ernest Lawrence Thayer

It looked extremely rocky for the Boston nine that day;
The score stood two to four, with but an inning left
to play.
So, when Cooney died at second, and Burrows did the
same,
A pallor wreathed the features of the patrons of the
game.

A straggling few got up to go, leaving there the rest,
With that hope which springs eternal within the human
breast.
For they thought: "If only Casey could get a whack
at that,"
They'd put even money now, with Casey at the bat.

But Flynn preceded Casey, and likewise so did Blake,
And the former was a pudd'n, and the latter was a
fake.
So on that stricken multitude a deathlike silence sat;
For there seemed but little chance of Casey's getting
to the bat.

But Flynn let drive a "single," to the wonderment of
all.

And the much-despised Blakey "tore the cover off the
ball."

And when the dust had lifted, and they saw what had
occurred,

There was Blakey safe at second, and Flynn a-huggin'
third.

Then from the gladdened multitude went up a joyous
yell—

It rumbled in the mountaintops, it rattled in the dell;

It struck upon the hillside and rebounded on the flat;

For Casey, mighty Casey, was advancing to the bat.

There was ease in Casey's manner as he stepped into
his place,

There was pride in Casey's bearing and a smile on
Casey's face;

And when responding to the cheers he lightly doffed
his hat,

No stranger in the crowd could doubt 'twas Casey at
the bat.

Ten thousand eyes were on him as he rubbed his hands
    with dirt,
Five thousand tongues applauded when he wiped them
    on his shirt;
Then when the writhing pitcher ground the ball into
    his hip,
Defiance glanced in Casey's eye, a sneer curled Casey's
    lip.

And now the leather-covered sphere came hurtling
    through the air,
And Casey stood a-watching it in haughty grandeur
    there.
Close by the sturdy batsman the ball unheeded sped;
"That ain't my style," said Casey. "Strike one," the
    umpire said.

From the benches, black with people, there went up a
    muffled roar,
Like the beating of the storm waves on the stern and
    distant shore.
"Kill him! kill the umpire!" shouted someone on the
    stand;
And it's likely they'd have killed him had not Casey
    raised his hand.

With a smile of Christian charity great Casey's visage
   shone;
He stilled the rising tumult, he made the game go on;
He signaled to the pitcher, and once more the spheroid
   flew;
But Casey still ignored it, and the umpire said, "Strike
   two."

"Fraud!" cried the maddened thousands, and the echo
   answered "Fraud!"
But one scornful look from Casey and the audience
   was awed; .
They saw his face grow stern and cold, they saw his
   muscles strain,
And they knew that Casey wouldn't let the ball go by
   again.

The sneer is gone from Casey's lips, his teeth are
   clenched in hate,
He pounds with cruel vengeance his bat upon the plate;
And now the pitcher holds the ball, and now he lets
   it go,
And now the air is shattered by the force of Casey's
   blow.

Oh, somewhere in this favored land the sun is shining
  bright,

The band is playing somewhere, and somewhere hearts
  are light;

And somewhere men are laughing, and somewhere
  children shout,

But there is no joy in Boston: Mighty Casey has struck
  out.

CASEY has been in the big league of poetry for a long time. That represents both his charm and his interpretive dangers. It is a warhorse that has been led to the pastures under the auspices of an actor whose florid style has frightened away most applicants for interpretation. There are some who scoff at Casey with the claim that he has struck out as a poem as well as a batsman. Judged as literature, the accusation can easily secure a conviction. But judged as a folk poem, it has as much validity as the game it depicts.

Rather than compare Thayer with Tennyson, one should compare Casey with Babe Ruth. The DeWolf Hopper pitch on this poem has been considered standard for so many years that we must impeach tradition to elect an acceptable performance. The secret to a good reading of this poem is enthusiasm. Like the Brooklyn Dodgers, Casey has that peculiar quality that fills the ball park with fans whose sneers are really cheers. "Come on, ya bum!" they shout, and pray to be proven wrong. You must love Casey or the poem can't possibly pay off. The key point occurs four lines from the end. Here all the frustration, the disgust, the misery, of the rabid fan must be brought to life. It is this stanza that validates the poem. More anon. Let us start at the beginning.

Let us designate this poem as farce. But remember that no farce ever succeeds unless all the parts are played "straight." If you laugh once at Casey or yourself, you've been shut out. You must treat the whole narration seriously—very seriously. Start this poem as though it were a baseball game. Warm up with a few easy throws. This will encompass the first three stanzas. This poem really starts off with a sigh; you have an unbearable burden; you're down in the dumps. Things don't look well at all.

At stanza four the umpire calls "play ball," and the action starts. Switch your delivery to that of a baseball announcer who excitedly tells you about Flynn's single and Blake's double. Start building the excitement in the fifth stanza. Build it up, up, up. Then break off sharply. The camera turns from the crowd for a closeup of Casey. Your voice is deeper, more intimate, has all the dignity of Casey, the sureness of his ability. Starting at the sixth stanza, have your reading in direct contrast to the preceding two blocks of rhyme.

In the eighth stanza, characterize Casey and the umpire— Casey aloof, the umpire in his time-honored fashion. The next stanza shifts the action to the stands. Try to get through the first two lines without pausing for breath. The third line calls for a duplication of the crowd's feelings. The next stanza is played like the fifth. The eleventh stanza parallels the treatment of the "kill the umpire" sequence. In the third line, read as though you were shouting with a lot of people and suddenly discovered that everybody was quiet but you, so you speak quietly, tensely. Then slowly build up, pyramid your intensity of reading and your volume through the next-to-last stanza. The highest peak of the poem is at this point. Take a long pause. Count seven slowly. Then start the last four lines.

As indicated above, this is the payoff stanza. The clue to success with it is the reading of the "Oh." This "Oh" is a cry of pain, deep, beaten, unhappy; it's the kind you get when somebody steps on your corn and the pain comes slow. Then read the rest of the stanza at a slower pace than the other part of the poem. You can't read it slowly enough. If you can put a slight break into your voice, it will help. Carry on until the colon and pause. Then, with all the anguish, disbelief, and horror that you can command, read "Mighty Casey . . . (pause) . . . has . . . (pause) . . . struck . . . (pause) out!"

ANNABEL LEE

Edgar Allan Poe

It was many and many a year ago,
　　In a kingdom by the sea,
That a maiden there lived, whom you may know
　　By the name of Annabel Lee;
And this maiden she lived with no other thought
　　Than to love, and be loved by me.

I was a child and she was a child,
　　In this kingdom by the sea;
But we loved with a love that was more than love,
　　I and my Annabel Lee,—
With a love that the wingèd seraphs of heaven
　　Coveted her and me.

And this was the reason that long ago,
　　In this kingdom by the sea,
A wind blew out of a cloud, chilling
　　My beautiful Annabel Lee;
So that her high-born kinsmen came,
　　And bore her away from me,
To shut her up in a sepulchre,
　　In this kingdom by the sea.

The angels, not so happy in heaven,
    Went envying her and me.
Yes! that was the reason (as all men know)
    In this kingdom by the sea,
That the wind came out of the cloud by night,
    Chilling and killing my Annabel Lee.

But our love it was stronger by far than the love
    Of those who were older than we,
    Of many far wiser than we;
And neither the angels in heaven above,
    Nor the demons down under the sea,
Can ever dissever my soul from the soul
    Of the beautiful Annabel Lee.

For the moon never beams without bringing me dreams
    Of the beautiful Annabel Lee,
And the stars never rise but I feel the bright eyes
    Of the beautiful Annabel Lee.
And so, all the night-tide I lie down by the side
Of my darling, my darling, my life, and my bride,
    In her sepulchre there by the sea,
    In her tomb by the sounding sea.

To surrender Poe and his work to the hands of the psychiatrists is a possible and suggested solution of the literary post-mortemers. The man who married a thirteen-year old girl, the confirmed alcoholic, the dismissed cadet from West Point may submit his life for Freudian investigation, but his poems are touched with his genius and, without arguing their quality, are splendid mood pieces for reading aloud.

Annabel Lee has all the minor key virtuosity of Tschaikowsky's symphonies and the appeal of the movie version of *Madame X*. It's a tear-jerker—pure and simple. But the reader who cries through his recitation will turn this ballad of sadness into a bar-room mellydrammer.

The dramatic problem that exists in this poem is in its first person singular form. You, the reader, must be Poe. It will be tempting to sob the tale, but the repression of the overflow of emotion can work out the reading into a successful result. Poe was a very unreal person; his whole life is an escape from reality. His miserable life was always accented with that touch of theatricalism that the critics decry, but which his parents (both actors) handed down to him. Like all actors, Poe has the need to dramatize himself. But if Poe was an actor, and you must play his part, let him be a good actor. Underplay the part instead of chewing up the scenery. "Annabel Lee" is not a poem, it is an emotional outburst. You must sympathize with the poet; you must appreciate his genuine despair. But you must keep it under control. Keep your reading reserved.

The rhyming scheme is not exact. It varies from stanza to stanza. Suppose you are Poe. It is dark outside; you are standing on a huge rock near a seacoast. The waves smash against the rock, and the spray soaks you. But you don't feel it. And then you hear a footstep. A sympathetic stranger comes, sits down beside you, recognizes your mood and, after waiting discreetly, asks you why you are sad. You have an understanding listener. And so you tell him your story. "It was many and many a year ago . . ."

In the last line of stanza one, pause after "love." Repeat this effect in the first line of stanza two after "child." In the fourth line of this stanza hold up after "I." Also in the sixth line after "her." This pattern exists throughout the poem.

In the third stanza Poe drops the role of story teller, and treats the situation more personally—this time with a touch of anger and resentment. This is not just another story; this is *my* story.

When we reach the last stanza, Poe has forgotten that he is telling this story to another person. He is completely wrapped up in himself. In the sixth line, you can be permitted one release of the emotional tension: in the second use of the phrase "my darling," it can be effective if you will let your voice crack just a bit. But then recovery should be quick. The last two lines are to be read slowly. In the last line, for example, put pauses after "tomb" and "sounding."

TO LUCASTA, ON GOING TO THE WARS
Richard Lovelace

Tell me not, Sweet, I am unkind
  That from the nunnery
Of thy chaste breast and quiet mind,
  To wars and arms I fly.

True, a new mistress now I chase,
  The first foe in the field;
And with a stronger faith embrace
  A sword, a horse, a shield.

Yet this inconstancy is such
  As you too shall adore;
I could not love thee, dear, so much,
  Loved I not honor more.

WHETHER it is the husband who tiptoes up the stairs at three A.M., shoes in hand after a card game with the boys, or the youngster who is lucidly alibi-ing his uninvited petty larceny of the cookie bowl, men of all ages and in all ages have been pretty good at excuses to their womenfolk. This poem is one of the best such excuses ever written. By admitting his eagerness to move onto other fields, the poet arms himself and disarms his lady. Why is he leaving her? Why, for her own sake, of course! The better to prove his love! What's more—she probably believed him.

Your reading of this poem will depend on the use to which you put the excuse. It is logical for a young lover, in explanation of a departure. It can be used by a young painter who gives up his job as a commercial artist and a steady salary to try his hand, like Gaugin, in the life of uncertainties of the South Seas. It fits many situations and your reading need not necessarily be anchored to the circumstances of the poet's original leaving to follow the royalist army into exile in France.

This is a gallant poem. It is the work of a cavalier poet in the seventeenth century. It is courtly and to be effective must be believable. One could burlesque the last two lines easily. However, by treating them with sincerity and simplicity, you'll probably make your point with ease.

The first line is a complete thought calling for a stop. The next three lines are treated as a unit. In the second stanza, hold "true" apart from the rest. In the last stanza, speak the "yet" logically and in the second line, bring the young lady in to share the decision by leaning on the word "too." In the last line, pause after "honor."

LIGHT SHINING OUT OF DARKNESS

William Cowper

God moves in a mysterious way
His wonders to perform;
He plants his footsteps in the sea,
And rides upon the storm.

Deep in unfathomable mines
Of never-failing skill
He treasures up his bright designs,
And works his sovereign will.

Ye fearful saints, fresh courage take!
The clouds ye so much dread
Are big with mercy, and shall break
In blessings on your head.

Judge not the Lord by feeble sense
But trust him for his grace;
Behind a frowning providence
He hides a smiling face.

His purposes will ripen fast,
   Unfolding every hour;
The bud may have a bitter taste,
   But sweet will be the flower.

Blind unbelief is sure to err,
   And scan his work in vain;
God is his own interpreter,
   And he will make it plain.

WHILE the first two lines of this poem are noted for their frequency of quotation, it is in the last two lines that the pivotal thought of this poem is set. This is a deeply religious piece that derives its impact, like the organ, from its slow, rolling pace. Keep the mood reverent, keep the pace measured, and avoid the danger of dullness by accenting all the verbs. A few samples: In line one, "moves"; in line seven, "treasures up"; in line eight, "works."

The accent need not necessarily be a louder tone. Emphasis is achieved in a variety of ways. A pause after the word to be emphasized sets the word apart and so creates a proper frame of emphasis. It is this time of accenting that is called for in this reading.

Whether by author's intent or printer's accident, it is important to consider "he" in the last line as though the "h" were capitalized. Underline this word in your reading; treat it with a capital letter. The sense of the poem will come into a clearer focus.

THE RUBAIYAT OF OMAR KHAYYAM
Edward Fitzgerald Translation

Come, fill the Cup, and in the fire of Spring
Your Winter-garment of Repentance fling:
   The Bird of Time has but a little way
To flutter—and the Bird is on the Wing.

Whether at Naishápúr or Babylon,
Whether the Cup with sweet or bitter run,
   The Wine of Life keeps oozing drop by drop,
The Leaves of Life keep falling one by one.

Each Morn a thousand Roses brings, you say;
Yes, but where leaves the Rose of Yesterday?
   And this first Summer month that brings the Rose
Shall take Jamshyd and Kaikobád away.

A Book of Verses underneath the Bough,
A Jug of Wine, a Loaf of Bread—and Thou
   Beside me singing in the Wilderness—
Oh, Wilderness were Paradise enow!

Some for the Glories of this World; and some
Sigh for the Prophet's Paradise to come;
   Ah, take the Cash, and let the Credit go,
Nor heed the rumble of a distant Drum!

And those who husbanded the Golden grain,
And those who flung it to the winds like Rain,
　　Alike to no such aureate Earth are turned
As, buried once, Men want dug up again.

The Worldly Hope men set their Hearts upon
Turns Ashes—or it prospers; and anon,
　　Like Snow upon the Desert's dusty Face,
Lighting a little hour or two—was gone.

I sometimes think that never blows so red
The Rose as where some buried Cæsar bled;
　　That every Hyacinth the Garden wears
Dropped in her lap from some once lovely Head.

And this reviving Herb whose tender Green
Fledges the River-Lip on which we lean—
　　Ah, lean upon it lightly! for who knows
From what once lovely Lip it springs unseen!

Ah, my Beloved, fill the Cup that clears
To-DAY of past Regret and future Fears:
　　To-MORROW!—Why, To-morrow I may be
Myself with Yesterday's Seven thousand Years.

For some we loved, the loveliest and the best
That from his Vintage rolling Time hath pressed,
   Have drunk their Cup a Round or two before,
And one by one crept silently to rest.

And we that now make merry in the Room
They left, and Summer dresses in new bloom,
   Ourselves must we beneath the Couch of Earth
Descend—ourselves to make a Couch—for whom?

Ah, make the most of what we yet may spend,
Before we too into the Dust descend;
   Dust into Dust, and under Dust, to lie,
Sans Wine, sans Song, sans Singer, and—sans End!

Alike for those who for To-DAY prepare,
And those that after some To-MORROW stare,
   A Muezzîn from the Tower of Darkness cries,
"Fools! your Reward is neither Here nor There!"

Myself when young did eagerly frequent
Doctor and Saint, and heard great argument
   About it and about: but evermore
Came out by the same door where in I went.

With them the seed of Wisdom did I sow,
And with mine own hand wrought to make it grow;
  And this was all the Harvest that I reaped—
"I came like Water, and like Wind I go."

Into this Universe, and *Why* not Knowing
Nor *Whence,* like Water willy-nilly flowing;
  And out of it, as Wind along the Waste,
I know not *Whither,* willy-nilly blowing.

What, without asking, hither hurried *Whence?*
And, without asking, *Whither* hurried hence!
  Oh, many a Cup of this forbidden Wine
Must drown the memory of that insolence!

Up from Earth's Center through the Seventh Gate
I rose, and on the Throne of Saturn sate,
  And many a Knot unraveled by the Road;
But not the Master-knot of Human Fate.

There was the Door to which I found no Key;
There was the Veil through which I might not see;
  Some little talk awhile of ME and THEE
There was—and then no more of THEE and ME.

Then to the Lip of this poor earthen Urn
I leaned, the Secret of my life to learn:
    And Lip to Lip it murmured—"While you live,
Drink!—for, once dead, you never shall return."

For I remember stopping by the way
To watch a Potter thumping his wet Clay:
    And with its all-obliterated Tongue
It murmured—"Gently, Brother, gently, pray!"

And has not such a Story from of Old
Down Man's successive generations rolled
    Of such a cloud of saturated Earth
Cast by the Maker into Human mold?

Perplexed no more with Human or Divine,
To-morrow's tangle to the winds resign,
    And lose your fingers in the tresses of
The Cypress-slender Minister of Wine.

And if the Wine you drink, the Lip you press,
End in what All begins and ends in—Yes;
    Think then you are To-DAY what YESTERDAY
You were—To-MORROW you shall not be less.

And fear not lest Existence closing your
Account, and mine, should know the like no more
  The Eternal Sákí from that Bowl has poured
Millions of Bubbles like us, and *will* pour.

When You and I behind the Veil are passed,
Oh, but the long, long while the World shall last,
  Which of our Coming and Departure heeds
As the Sea's self should heed a pebble-cast.

A Moment's Halt—a momentary taste
Of BEING from the Well amid the Waste—
  And Lo!—the phantom Caravan has reached
The NOTHING it set out from—Oh, make haste!

But if in vain, down on the stubborn floor
Of Earth, and up to Heaven's unopening Door,
  You gaze TO-DAY, while You are You—how then
TO-MORROW, You when shall be You no more?

Waste not your Hour, nor in the vain pursuit
Of This and That endeavor and dispute;
  Better be jocund with the fruitful Grape
Than sadden after none, or bitter, Fruit.

Ah, but my Computations, People say,
Reduced the Year to better reckoning?—Nay,
   'Twas only striking from the Calendar
Unborn To-morrow, and dead Yesterday.

Oh threats of Hell and Hopes of Paradise!
One thing at least is certain—*This* Life flies:
   One thing is certain and the rest is Lies;
The Flower that once has blown for ever dies.

Strange, is it not? that of the myriads who
Before us passed the door of Darkness through,
   Not one returns to tell us of the Road,
Which to discover we must travel too.

I sent my Soul through the Invisible
Some letter of that After-life to spell:
   And by and by my Soul returned to me,
And answered, "I Myself am Heaven and Hell."

Heaven but the Vision of fulfilled Desire,
And Hell the Shadow from a Soul on fire
   Cast on the Darkness into which Ourselves
So late emerged from, shall so soon expire.

We are no other than a moving row
Of Magic Shadow-shapes that come and go
Round with the Sun-illumined Lantern held
In Midnight by the Master of the Show;

But helpless Pieces of the Game He plays
Upon this Checker-board of Nights and Days;
Hither and thither moves, and checks, and slays,
And one by one back in the Closet lays.

The Ball no question makes of Ayes and Noes,
But Here or There, as strikes the Player, goes;
And He that tossed you down into the Field,
He knows about it all—HE knows—HE knows!

The Moving Finger writes; and, having writ,
Moves on: nor all your Piety nor Wit
Shall lure it back to cancel half a Line
Nor all your Tears wash out a Word of it.

And that inverted Bowl they call the Sky,
Whereunder crawling cooped we live and die,
Lift not your hands to *It* for help—for It
As impotently moves as you or I.

With Earth's first Clay They did the Last Man knead,
And there of the Last Harvest sowed the Seed;
   And the first Morning of Creation wrote
What the Last Dawn of Reckoning shall read.

YESTERDAY *This* Day's Madness did prepare;
TO-MORROW'S Silence, Triumph, or Despair:
   Drink! for you know not whence you came, nor why:
Drink! for you know not why you go, nor where.

Yon rising Moon that looks for us again—
How oft hereafter will she wax and wane;
   How oft hereafter rising look for us
Through this same Garden—and for *one* in vain!

And when like her, oh Sákí, you shall pass
Among the Guests Star-scattered on the Grass,
   And in your joyous errand reach the spot
Where I made One—turn down an empty Glass!

OMAR KHAYYAM was the Dale Carnegie of his day, with a recipe for peace of mind. The Rubáiyát is Mr. Carnegie's permanent best-seller (*How To Stop Worrying and Start Living*) in a lusher setting and in poetic form.

Omar is a man who has accepted the inevitable—forgotten the past and disdained the future. He is a practical man, or rather, philosopher, who doesn't know where he came from or where he is going—but is absolutely convinced that he can't go wrong taking a profit. He is not disturbed, as so many readings tend to index him. He's completely at peace with himself.

You can read into his quatrains all the mysticisms of the East that you wish. But the exotic setting of his masterpiece has often lured readers into a pose that finds their voices sitting on a magic carpet and their spirit vaguely smoking an oriental hookah. Check into Omar's works, call him by his first name, get friendly with his verses instead of salaaming before you read them. There has been too general a tendency to stand away and admire the Rubaiyat rather than to apply the philosophy to modern-day living.

You can paint the quatrain that starts "The Moving Finger . . ." with the colors found on the palette of an oriental miniature. Or—you can rephrase it and say, "What's the use of worrying?" as did Mr. Carnegie.

In other words, this is no poem to approach through the squeaky and mysterious door of the *Inner Sanctum.* This is no piece played in a minor key. But it is the literary celebration of a man who is determined to live each day to its fullest. That is a rather positive philosophy, and you should treat it as such.

The standard treatment of this poem (check your memory) is to read it *mysterioso* with a background of music selected from the *Scheherezade Suite* of Rimsky-Korsakoff and to give a touch of sinister threat to each statement. But instead of reading these quatrains with a warning finger, try interpreting them with a shrug of your shoulder. In that "Moving Finger" quatrain, for instance, which is very well known, isn't Omar's meaning really, "What's done, is done?"

Go through the poem and fit present day colloquialisms against each Persian picture. It's an interesting exercise. As a man who was in love with today, Mr. Omar certainly would not approve of our looking back upon him in the past but would prefer to have us bring him up to date that way. This does not mean that we must turn his verse into slang. But certainly his thoughts, by their very nature, are entitled to a colloquial cloak.

Flowing through the poem, and at a rapid pace, are magnums of the vineyards' produce. While we do not wish to dispute Mr. Omar's weakness for the jug, we should like to suggest to the interpreter the possibility of the wine's being in actuality a symbolism for living on a cash basis. The wine is Omar's trademark and must be considered part of his philosophy rather than a part of his diet.

THE SAD TALE OF MR. MEARS

Unknown

There was a man who had a clock,
His name was Matthew Mears;
And <u>every</u> day he wound that clock
For eight and twenty years.

And then one day he found that clock
An <u>eight</u>-day clock to be,
And a madder man than Matthew Mears
You would not wish to see.

AFTER some of the feature-length productions in this volume, this rates as a short subject, put in for change of pace. Underline the word "every" in the third line and "eight" in the sixth line.

THE SPIDER AND THE FLY
A Fable

Mary Howitt

"Will you walk into my parlor?" said the spider to the
    fly;
" 'Tis the prettiest little parlor that ever you did spy.
The way into my parlor is up a winding stair,
And I have many pretty things to show when you are
    there."
"O no, no," said the little fly, "to ask me is in vain,
For who goes up your winding stair can ne'er come
    down again."

"I'm sure you must be weary, dear, with soaring up
    so high;
Will you rest upon my little bed?" said the spider to
    the fly.
There are pretty curtains drawn around, the sheets are
    fine and thin,
And if you like to rest awhile, I'll snugly tuck you in."
"O no, no," said the little fly, "for I've often heard
    it said,
They *never, never wake* again, who sleep upon *your*
    bed."

Said the cunning spider to the fly, "Dear friend, what
   shall I do,
To prove the warm affection I've always felt for you?
I have within my pantry good store of all that's nice;
I'm sure you're very welcome; will you please to take
   a slice?"
"O no, no," said the little fly, "kind sir, that cannot
   be;
I've heard what's in your pantry, and I do not wish
   to see."

"Sweet creature!" said the spider, "you're witty and
   you're wise,
How handsome are your gauzy wings, how brilliant are
   your eyes!
I have a little looking-glass upon my parlor shelf,
If you'll step in one moment, dear, you shall behold
   yourself."
"I thank you, gentle sir," she said, "for what you're
   pleased to say,
And bidding you good-morning *now,* I'll call *another*
   day."

The spider turned him round about, and went into his
den,
For well he knew the silly fly would soon be back again:
So he wove a subtle web, in a little corner sly,
And set his table ready to dine upon the fly.
Then he came out to his door again, and merrily did
sing,
"Come hither, hither, pretty fly, with the pearl and
silver wing:
Your robes are green and purple; there's a crest upon
your head;
Your eyes are like the diamond bright, but mine are
dull as lead."

Alas, alas! how very soon this silly little fly,
Hearing his wily flattering words, came slowly flitting
by.
With buzzing wings she hung aloft, then near and
nearer drew,
Thinking only of her brilliant eyes, and green and
purple hue;
Thinking only of her crested head—*poor foolish thing!*
At last,

Up jumped the cunning spider, and fiercely held her
fast.

He dragged her up his winding stair, into his dismal
den,

Within his little parlor; but she ne'er came out again!

And now, dear little children, who may this story read,

To idle, silly, flattering words, I pray you ne'er give
heed;

Unto an evil counselor close heart, and ear, and eye,

And take a lesson from this tale of the Spider and the
Fly.

EVERY good father, like every good doctor, is expected to have a good bedside manner. This refers not so much to his curative powers, but to his histrionic ability. While this is a lesson for adults, it is a poem for children. The Spider and the Fly are a fairly melodramatic Samson and Delilah, or to put them in the parallel order, Delilah and Samson. In the movies one would immediately typecast Jerry Colonna as the spider and any vain and vacuous blonde as the fly.

From the perspective of childhood it is expected that the adult reading the poem will characterize the two protagonists broadly. You must twirl your mustaches when you are acting out the spider, and you must convey the silly smugness of the fly by assuming a simpering tone.

At the sixth line of the third stanza from the end, you are permitted the florid reading of the flattering lines.

In the second stanza from the end, you, as the reader, become part of the story. You are the commentator on the scene, the radio announcer describing a special event. As the stanza develops, accelerate the excitement. This is necessary both for proper dramatic values and for the proper contrast to the last stanza.

The closing four lines are the moral. They must be read slowly, so that the thought will sink in. Read against the pattern of the description of the trap, this common sense comes into proper focus.

THE DAY IS DONE

Henry Wadsworth Longfellow

The day is done, and the darkness
    Falls from the wings of Night,
As a feather is wafted downward
    From an eagle in his flight.

I see the lights of the village
    Gleam through the rain and the mist,
And a feeling of sadness comes o'er me
    That my soul cannot resist:

A feeling of sadness and longing,
    That is not akin to pain,
And resembles sorrow only
    As the mist resembles the rain.

Come, read to me some poem,
    Some simple and heartfelt lay,
That shall soothe this restless feeling,
    And banish the thoughts of day.

Not from the grand old masters,
  Not from the bards sublime,
Whose distant footsteps echo
  Through the corridors of Time.

For, like strains of martial music,
  Their mighty thoughts suggest
Life's endless toil and endeavor;
  And tonight I long for rest.

Read from some humbler poet,
  Whose songs gushed from his heart,
As showers from the clouds of summer,
  Or tears from the eyelids start;

Who, through long days of labor,
  And nights devoid of ease,
Still heard in his soul the music
  Of wonderful melodies.

Such songs have power to quiet
   The restless pulse of care,
And come like the benediction
   That follows after prayer.

Then read from the treasured volume
   The poem of thy choice,
And lend to the rhyme of the poet
   The beauty of thy voice.

And the night shall be filled with music,
   And the cares, that infest the day,
Shall fold their tents, like the Arabs,
   And as silently steal away.

THE reading direction is in the title of this piece. It is quiet and relaxed. The rhyming scheme shows the second and fourth line of each stanza is parallel. This, combined with the exact rhythm, poses a problem in preventing a sing-song reading. This can be handled by treating the poem not by stanzas but by images.

For example, in the first line, "The day is done" rates a solo position, whereas the rest of the stanza is properly run together. The second and third stanzas are a unified thought and should be kept together. The fourth, fifth, and sixth can come together.

When reading the last lines, suspend the words so they do not resolve in a completed thought. This does not mean a rising inflection, but rather a sort of holding on to the sound, and starting the next sentence on top of the overtones created by holding on to the preceding words. Stanzas seven and eight are a unit. Nine is a development of the eighth stanza but is an image by itself. The last two stanzas bring the poem to a finish that parallels the quiet note sounded in the opening phrase.

ALL THE WORLD'S A STAGE

William Shakespeare

All the world's a stage
And all the men and women merely players:
They have their exits and their entrances;
And one man in his time plays many parts,
His acts being seven ages. At first the infant,
Mewling and puking in the nurse's arms.
Then the whining school-boy, with his satchel
And shining morning face, creeping like snail
Unwillingly to school. And then the lover,
Sighing like furnace, with a woeful ballad
Made to his mistress' eyebrow. Then a soldier,
Full of strange oaths, and bearded like the pard,
Jealous in honor, sudden and quick in quarrel,
Seeking the bubble reputation
Even in the cannon's mouth. And then the justice,
In fair round belly with good capon lined,
With eyes severe and beard of formal cut,
Full of wise saws and modern instances;
And so he plays his part. The sixth age shifts
Into the lean and slippered pantaloon,

With spectacles on nose and pouch on side,
His youthful hose, well saved, a world too wide
For his shrunk shank; and his big manly voice,
Turning again toward childish treble, pipes
And whistles in his sound. Last scene of all,
That ends this strange eventful history,
Is second childishness and mere oblivion,
Sans teeth, sans eyes, sans taste, sans every thing.

(*from* AS YOU LIKE IT)

THE actor Shakespeare has provided a perfect showpiece for Shakespeare's actors. One could easily imagine this as the standard audition piece for entrance into the Globe Theatre Company. In a sense this is the sequel to Shakespeare's advice to the players in *Hamlet*—a test to determine how well the lesson has been received.

But it's more than an actor's holiday; it's a diagram of life. This reading is specifically for those of advanced training. It is a *tour de force*. One must be an infant, one must whine like a schoolboy, and follow the passages of the piece to toothless old age. Since this is an interpolated bit, like the singing lesson in *The Barber of Seville,* one may readily take it from the context of the play that spawned it and treat it as a separate unit that stands on its own feet.

Move into this easily, like a pitcher warming up on the mound in advance of the pyrotechnics that he reserves for the duel with the batter. The virtuosity starts with the cataloguing of the ages. Treat each stage as though you were actually going through it. Set your rhythms to match the age you portray; the justice, for example, must be slower, weightier, fatter.

Pay particular attention to the enunciation of "every thing." They are two separate words. Treat them in that fashion.

ABOU BEN ADHEM

James Henry Leigh Hunt

Abou Ben Adhem (may his tribe increase!)
Awoke one night from a deep dream of peace,
And saw, within the moonlight in his room,
Making it rich, and like a lily in bloom,
An Angel writing in a book of gold:
Exceeding peace had made Ben Adhem bold,
And to the Presence in the room he said,
"What writest thou?" The vision raised its head,
And with a look made of all sweet accord
Answered, "The names of those who love the Lord."
"And is mine one?" said Abou. "Nay, not so,"
Replied the Angel. Abou spoke more low,
But cheerily still; and said, "I pray thee, then,
Write me as one that loves his fellow men."

The Angel wrote, and vanished. The next night
It came again with a great wakening light,
And showed the names whom love of God had blessed,
And, lo! Ben Adhem's name led all the rest!

THE rhyming scheme here is so hypnotic that the temptation to roll the rhythm around in the neatly shaped container of words might lead one to admire the bottle but not the contents.

Exploring the meaning of this oft repeated piece is necessary to proper interpretation. Here was a man, Abou Ben Adhem, who was not labelled in the formal index of religious practices. Yet, when a showdown came, he rested his case on his love for his fellowman rather than his love for the Lord. The moral is that loving one's fellowman is a practical way of loving the Lord.

In reading this poem, don't fall into the trap of the rhyming scheme. Follow the punctuation marks of *thought* carefully. This will help break up the constant rhythm, which makes for a dull rendition. In the fifth and sixth lines, the words "gold" and "bold" rhyme, but there is no connecting thought. They must, therefore, be separated. Hunt provides the punctuation to guide you in alchemizing the written word into the spoken word.

THE HEIGHT OF THE RIDICULOUS
Oliver Wendell Holmes

I wrote some lines once on a time
  In wondrous merry mood,
And thought, as usual, men would say
  They were exceeding good.

They were so queer, so very queer,
  I laughed as I would die;
Albeit, in the general way,
  A sober man am I.

I called my servant, and he came;
  How kind it was of him
To mind a slender man like me,
  He of the mighty limb!

"These to the printer," I exclaimed,
  And, in my humorous way,
I added (as a trifling jest),
  "There'll be the devil to pay."

He took the paper, and I watched,
   And saw him peep within;
At the first line he read, his face
   Was all upon the grin.

He read the next; the grin grew broad,
   And shot from ear to ear;
He read the third; a chuckling noise
   I now began to hear.

The fourth; he broke into a roar;
   The fifth; his waistband split;
The sixth; he burst five buttons off,
   And tumbled in a fit.

Ten days and nights, with sleepless eye,
   I watched that wretched man,
And since, I never dare to write
   As funny as I can.

THERE are two servants to be dealt with in this piece. The first appears in the poem and the second is you. In any final analysis, a reader must be the servant of the creator. The response of the first is the warning to the second.

While the servant in the poem responds in an uproarious manner, any such treatment by the second servant would destroy the texture of this poem. Holmes is no Bob Hope, his humor isn't the "hit-em-on-the-head, roll-em-in-the-aisles" type. While this isn't a funny poem, it *is* a poem for fun. The simplicity is deceiving. One of the most difficult of all interpretive problems is found in the alleyways of comedy. The line of demarcation between clowns and wits may be sharply defined and easily handled, but the shades of difference in between are serious challenges.

"The Height of the Ridiculous" is a case in point. The author pokes fun—at you, himself, at his servant, at comedy writers. He does this gently. Some of the humor is wide-eyed: exhibit, stanza three. Some of it is a pun, the reference to printers and devils. (A "printer's devil" was a young apprentice, a type-setter for the printer. Traditionally, he is represented as a lad always covered with inky soot and always bearing the brunt of the printer's displeasure and mistakes.) All in all it may perhaps be best to give this a broad treatment—a sort of broken field running that helps score touchdowns on the gridiron.

The element of timing is vital. The right pause at the right place is necessary. For example, in the third line the words "as usual" recited "straight" carry an immodest flavor, yet by emphasizing them properly, they take on an amusing color. Again in the second stanza, the first two lines are best read "straight" but then one must switch pace for the last two. Study this poem for a while; you will realize that the comic values come from the "asides." For example, in the fourth stanza, the last three lines are an "aside." It is as though the author is saying, "Don't take me seriously. I'm really fooling."

In the fifth stanza, Holmes has compiled an inventory of hearty laughter. He treats each step as a "still" in a picture story in one of our national magazines. He even numbers them. Treat them separately and build one on top of the other.

The last stanza is apart from the rest. Here the humor evolves from the sadness of the reading.

THE CONSTANT LOVER

Sir John Suckling

Out upon it, I have loved
  Three whole days together!
And am like to love three more,
  If it prove fair weather.

Time shall moult away his wings
  Ere he shall discover
In the whole wide world again
  Such a constant lover.

But the spite on't is, no praise
  Is due at all to me:
Love with me had made no stays,
  Had it been but she.

Had it any been but she,
  And that very face,
There had been at least ere this
  A dozen in her place.

THIS lover has pledged the devotion of a lifetime and confirmed it by a run of three consecutive days. What's more, he's willing to concede an additional trio of twenty-four hours. While this hardly smacks of permanence, it is easily recognized as the apology of a confirmed Don Juan who feels that the average woman should be prosecuted under the Sherman antitrust monopoly act.

One cannot take this poem too seriously. It is a romantic piece that belongs both in language and spirit to a Douglas Fairbanks, wrapped in the costume of the seventeen hundreds with a sword dangling at his side. One should decide immediately that the reader is making fun of himself. The writing is such that one cannot give it a contemporary flavor. It is a costume piece in technicolor and must be treated as such.

In bringing this poem to life, give it a spontaneous reading. The poet is exuberant. Perhaps you will succeed with this one best if you treat it in the manner that certain contemporary singers like Beatrice Kay handle the ballads of the Gay Nineties with good singing, but just a touch of kidding.

Make up your mind that this is not a love poem but a comic poem and you'll have fun with it.

THE RAVEN
Edgar Allan Poe

Once upon a midnight dreary, while I pondered, weak
and weary,
Over many a quaint and curious volume of forgotten
lore—
While I nodded, nearly napping, suddenly there came
a tapping,
As of some one gently rapping, rapping at my chamber
door.
" 'Tis some visitor," I muttered, "tapping at my
chamber door;
> Only this, and nothing more."

Ah, distinctly I remember, it was in the bleak De-
cember,
And each separate dying ember wrought its ghost upon
the floor.
Eagerly I wished the morrow; vainly I had sought to
borrow
From my books surcease of sorrow—sorrow for the
lost Lenore—
For the rare and radiant maiden whom the angels
name Lenore—
> Nameless here forevermore.

And the silken, sad, uncertain rustling of each purple
    curtain
Thrilled me—filled me with fantastic terrors never
    felt before;
So that now, to still the beating of my heart, I stood
    repeating,
" 'Tis some visitor entreating entrance at my chamber
    door;
Some late visitor entreating entrance at my chamber
    door;
        That it is, and nothing more."

Presently my soul grew stronger; hesitating then no
    longer,
"Sir," said I, "or madam, truly your forgiveness I
    implore;
But the fact is, I was napping, and so gently you came
    rapping,
And so faintly you came tapping, tapping at my cham-
    ber door,
That I scarce was sure I heard you."—Here I opened
    wide the door;
        Darkness there, and nothing more.

Deep into that darkness peering, long I stood there,
wondering, fearing,
Doubting, dreaming dreams no mortal ever dared to
dream before;
But the silence was unbroken, and the darkness gave
no token,
And the only word there spoken was the whispered
word "Lenore!"
This I whispered, and an echo murmured back the
word "Lenore!"
Merely this, and nothing more.

Back into the chamber turning, all my soul within me
burning,
Soon again I heard a tapping, something louder than
before:
"Surely," said I, "surely that is something at my
window-lattice;
Let me see then what thereat is, and this mystery
explore—
Let my heart be still a moment, and this mystery
explore;
'Tis the wind, and nothing more."

Open then I flung the shutter, when, with many a
flirt and flutter,
In there stepped a stately raven of the saintly days of
yore.
Not the least obeisance made he; not an instant stopped
or stayed he;
But, with mien of lord or lady, perched above my
chamber door—
Perched upon a bust of Pallas, just above my chamber
door—
> Perched, and sat, and nothing more.

Then this ebony bird beguiling my sad fancy into
smiling,
By the grave and stern decorum of the countenance it
wore,
"Though thy crest be shorn and shaven, thou," I said,
"art sure no craven;
Ghastly, grim, and ancient raven, wandering from the
nightly shore,
Tell me what thy lordly name is on the night's Plu-
tonian shore?"
> Quoth the raven, "Nevermore!"

Much I marvelled this ungainly fowl to hear discourse
  so plainly,
Though its answer little meaning, little relevancy bore;
For we cannot help agreeing that no living human
  being
Ever yet was blessed with seeing bird above his chamber door,
Bird or beast upon the sculptured bust above his
  chamber door,
        With such name as "Nevermore!"

But the raven, sitting lonely on the placid bust, spoke
  only
That one word, as if his soul in that one word he did
  outpour.
Nothing further then he uttered, not a feather then
  he fluttered—
Till I scarcely more than muttered, "Other friends
  have flown before.
On the morrow he will leave me, as my hopes have
  flown before."
        Then the bird said, "Nevermore!"

Startled at the stillness, broken by reply so aptly
  spoken,
"Doubtless," said I, "what it utters is its only stock
  and store,
Caught from some unhappy master, whom unmerciful
  disaster
Followed fast and followed faster, till his song one
  burden bore,
Till the dirges of his hope that melancholy burden
  bore,—
          Of 'Never, nevermore!' "

But the raven still beguiling all my sad soul into
  smiling,
Straight I wheeled a cushioned seat in front of bird
  and bust and door,
Then, upon the velvet sinking, I betook myself to
  linking
Fancy unto fancy, thinking what this ominous bird of
  yore—
What this grim, ungainly, ghastly, gaunt, and ominous
  bird of yore—
          Meant in croaking "Nevermore!"

This I sat engaged in guessing, but no syllable expressing
To the fowl whose fiery eyes now burned into my
bosom's core;
This and more I sat divining, with my head at ease
reclining
On the cushion's velvet lining that the lamplight
gloated o'er,
But whose velvet violet lining, with the lamplight
gloating o'er,
   She shall press—ah! nevermore!

Then methought the air grew denser, perfumed from
an unseen censer,
Swung by seraphim, whose footfalls tinkled on the
tufted floor.
"Wretch," I cried, "thy God hath lent thee—by these
angels he hath sent thee
Respite—respite and nepenthe from my memories of
Lenore!
Quaff, O, quaff this kind nepenthe, and forget this lost
Lenore!"
   Quoth the raven, "Nevermore!"

"Prophet!" said I, "thing of evil!—prophet still, if bird
or devil!

Whether tempter sent, or whether tempest tossed thee
here ashore,

Desolate yet all undaunted, on this desert land enchanted,

On this home by horror haunted—tell me truly, I
implore—

Is there—is there balm in Gilead?—tell me, tell me,
I implore!"

          Quoth the raven, "Nevermore!"

"Prophet!" said I, "thing of evil!—prophet still, if bird
or devil!

By that heaven that bends above us—by that God
we both adore,

Tell this soul with sorrow laden, if, within the distant
Aidenn,

It shall clasp a sainted maiden, whom the angels name
Lenore,

Clasp a fair and radiant maiden, whom the angels
name Lenore!"

          Quoth the raven, "Nevermore!"

"Be that word our sign of parting, bird or fiend!" I
shrieked, upstarting—
"Get thee back into the tempest and the night's Plu-
tonian shore!
Leave no black plume as a token of that lie thy soul
hath spoken!
Leave my loneliness unbroken!—quit the bust above
my door!
Take thy beak from out my heart, and take thy form
from off my door!"
        Quoth the raven, "Nevermore!"

And the raven, never flitting, still is sitting, still is
sitting
On the pallid bust of Pallas, just above my chamber
door;
And his eyes have all the seeming of a demon that
is dreaming,
And the lamplight o'er him streaming throws his
shadow on the floor;
And my soul from out that shadow that lies floating
on the floor
        Shall be lifted—*nevermore!*

"THE RAVEN" is an autobiographical poem. Checking the facts of Poe's life against the contents of this poem is both a confirmation and interpretive assist. A chronic alcoholic, Poe followed the pattern so exactly that in his poem he hid the bottle and called it a book, as though ashamed to admit his inebriation. We can easily imagine Poe rationalizing his drinking as a necessary aid to his writing. His gallery of heroines— Annabel, Helen, Lenore—can be matched up with specific women in his life as a sort of literary parlor game.

This whole poem is a form of delirium tremens. It is *The Lost Weekend* set to rhyme. Some alcoholics see pink elephants; Poe visualized a dark Raven. And since the Raven is not a bird, what is its symbolism?

All manner of theories have been advanced, and many are acceptable. It is a fascinating game, and a necessary conclusion before you start to turn these written words into spoken words. Is the Raven a symbol of Poe's conscience? Is it a representation to him of Satan? Is it the temptation of drink? I rather suspect that it's all of these and more. As you study the poem you will realize that Poe reacts to it differently throughout. The confusion is natural in an alcoholic haze.

The second challenge is in the interpretation of the "Nevermore." As you proceed you find that it has different values at different times. Perhaps it represents the essence of "The Negative," that unhappy ending that fate seems to have transfused into all Poe's actions.

If you will go along with the annotator on his interpretative assumption that this is a description and reaction to a alcoholic interlude, the pieces of the poem will fit in together This would make the reading an exhausting experience. The tricky rhyming scheme carries the poem along for the reader but at no time must you let the poem control you. You must hold on to it with a firm hand and voice. In the last thi of the piece, Poe rants and raves against the Raven. You will dilute the effectiveness of the reading by moving with the flow of the poem. The proper effect is created by intensity rather than by volume. Try it! Take the fourth stanza from the end. Read it first in a shouting manner. Then read it again; this time with quiet intensity. You'll know you're hitting it on the head when you feel it in the pit of your stomach.

As a general tone for the entire reading, set the stage for yourself in your mind's eye. It is midnight, it is quiet, it is dark, you're tired. You won't use full voice at any stage of the reading. This is a mood piece and a long one. You couldn't possibly shout your way through it. Speak softly, use a breathy quality in your voice and remember—you're scared!

By treating the Raven as an imagined symbol instead of an actual bird, you will keep your reading in the context of the fantasy of the situation.

Exact instructions for emphasis would be ridiculous for this work. If you follow the basic concept, and work over Poe's rhymes and punctuations, it will all fit together. Watch for the rhymes within the body of the stanza. In the third, for instance, we find "thrilled me" and "filled me." Later on we see "beating," "repeating," "entreating."

A few words that may be strange to you: seraphim—angels; nepenthe (accent on 'pen')—a drink that helps one forget.

The characterization of the Raven remains constant throughout. Poe changes, wheedles, fights, retreats, but the Raven is immobile. It is actually Poe's bombardment of the Raven, approaching it from every angle, trying to get a different reaction from it, trying to get it under his control that activates the conflict in this poem. It is the unshaken position of the Raven that drives Poe to fury and finally leaves him as we find him in the last stanza—weak, exhausted, a man who has surrendered—to the Raven.

SONG

Henry Wadsworth Longfellow

Stay, stay at home, my heart, and rest;
Home-keeping hearts are happiest,
For those that wander they know not where
Are full of trouble and full of care;
　　To stay at home is best.

Weary and homesick and distressed,
They wander east, they wander west,
And are baffled and beaten and blown about
By the winds of the wilderness of doubt;
　　To stay at home is best.

Then stay at home, my heart, and rest;
The bird is safest in its nest;
O'er all that flutter their wings and fly
A hawk is hovering in the sky;
　　To stay at home is best.

WITHOUT an accompanying byline, one would hesitate between assigning this poem to H. W. Longfellow or E. A. Guest. It is much more quotable than notable.

The fifth line in each grouping is not a fifth wheel at all. Rather, it is to the treatment of this fifth line that you should assign the bulk of your interpretive attention; the rest takes care of itself in a simple rhythm and simple rhyming scheme. In the first two stanzas, the treatment should be the same— by not resolving the thought at the end of the fourth lines you attach the fifth to the body of the stanza. In the last set, however, resolve the fourth line, take a seat, then read the closing line.

LOCHINVAR

Sir Walter Scott

Oh, young Lochinvar is come out of the west:
Through all the wide border his steed was the best;
And save his good broadsword he weapons had none;
He rode all unarmed and he rode all alone.
So faithful in love, and so dauntless in war,
There never was knight like the young Lochinvar!

He stayed not for brake, and he stopped not for stone;
He swam the Esk River where ford there was none:
But ere he alighted at Netherby gate,
The bride had consented, the gallant came late;
For a laggard in love, and a dastard in war,
Was to wed the fair Ellen of brave Lochinvar.

So boldly he entered the Netherby Hall,
Among bridesmen, and kinsmen, and brothers, and all:
Then spoke the bride's father, his hand on his sword
(For the poor craven bridegroom said never a word),
"O come ye in peace here, or come ye in war,
Or to dance at our bridal, young Lord Lochinvar?"

"I long wooed your daughter, my suit you denied;—
Love swells like the Solway, but ebbs like its tide!
And now am I come, with this lost love of mine,
To lead but one measure, drink one cup of wine:
There are maidens in Scotland more lovely by far,
That would gladly be bride to the young Lochinvar."

The bride kissed the goblet: the knight took it up,
He quaffed of the wine, and he threw down the cup.
She looked down to blush, and she looked up to sigh,
With a smile on her lips, and a tear in her eye.
He took her soft hand, ere her mother could bar—
"Now tread we a measure!" said young Lochinvar.

So stately his form, and so lovely her face,
That never a hall such a galliard did grace:
While her mother did fret, and her father did fume,
And the bridegroom stood dangling his bonnet and
    plume;
And the bride-maidens whispered, " 'Twere better by far
To have matched our fair cousin with young Loch-
    invar."

One touch to her hand, and one word in her ear,
When they reached the hall door, and the charger
    stood near;
So light to the croupe the fair lady he swung,
So light to the saddle before her he sprung!
"She is won! we are gone, over bank, bush, and scaur:
They'll have fleet steeds that follow," quoth young
    Lochinvar.

There was mounting 'mong Graemes of the Netherby
    clan:
Forsters, Fenwicks, and Musgraves, they rode and they
    ran;
There was racing and chasing on Canobie Lee,
But the lost bride of Netherby ne'er did they see.
So daring in love, and so dauntless in war,
Have ye e'er heard of gallant like young Lochinvar?

                                        (*from* MARMION)

THE setting may be Scotland, but the pace and action are more reminiscent of a western "opera" turned out by an independent producer amidst the rough terrain of the Hollywoods. It has everything that one would expect from this type of production: a chase, horses, arms –and there is even a pause in the wedding scene for the typical musical interlude.

Naturally, one must approach this piece with a swagger. The mood is strong, dashing, energetic. Lochinvar is Hopalong Cassidy dressed in kilts.

Action is the keynote of this poem. Set a fast pace and keep it going until the first break occurs after the colon in the second line of the third stanza. There is a suspenseful pause; the members of the wedding party await Lochinvar's statement of intention. The quotations of the father are measured and slow and nervous compared to the sturdiness of Lochinvar. If you own a Scotch burr, characterize the speech. But play it lightly—don't overdo it. The pace picks up in the fourth stanza, and accelerates into high gear in the last stanza.

THE BRIDGE OF SIGHS
Thomas Hood

One more Unfortunate,
Weary of breath,
Rashly importunate,
Gone to her death!

Take her up tenderly,
Lift her with care:
Fashion'd so slenderly,
Young, and so fair.

Look at her garments
Clinging like cerements;
Whilst the wave constantly
Drips from her clothing;
Take her up instantly,
Loving, not loathing.

Touch her not scornfully;
Think of her mournfully,
Gently and humanly;
Not of the stains of her,
All that remains of her
Now is pure womanly.

Make no deep scrutiny
Into her mutiny
Rash and undutiful:
Past all dishonour,
Death has left on her
Only the beautiful.

Still, for all slips of hers,
One of Eve's family—
Wipe those poor lips of hers
Oozing so clammily.

Loop up her tresses
Escaped from the comb,
Her fair auburn tresses;
Whilst wonderment guesses
Where was her home?

Who was her father?
Who was her mother?
Had she a sister?
Had she a brother?
Or was there a dearer one
Still, and a nearer one
Yet, than all others?

Alas! for the rarity
Of Christian charity
Under the sun!
O, it was pitiful!
Near a whole city full,
Home she had none!

Sisterly, brotherly,
Fatherly, motherly
Feelings had changed:
Love, by harsh evidence,
Thrown from its eminence;
Even God's providence
Seeming estranged.

Where the lamps quiver
So far in the river,
With many a light
From window and casement,
From garret to basement,
She stood, with amazement,
Houseless by night.

The bleak wind of March
Made her tremble and shiver;
But not the dark arch,
Or the black flowing river:
Mad from life's history,
Glad to death's mystery,
Swift to be hurl'd—
Anywhere, anywhere
Out of the world!

In she plunged boldly—
No matter how coldly
The rough river ran—
Over the brink of it,
Picture it—think of it,
Dissolute Man!
Lave in it, drink of it,
Then, if you can!

Take her up tenderly,
Lift her with care;
Fashion'd so slenderly,
Young, and so fair!

Ere her limbs frigidly
Stiffen too rigidly,
Decently, kindly,
Smooth and compose them;
And her eyes, close them,
Staring so blindly!

Dreadfully staring
Thro' muddy impurity,
As when with the daring
Last look of despairing
Fix'd on futurity.

Perishing gloomily,
Spurr'd by contumely,
Cold inhumanity,
Burning insanity,
Into her rest.—
Cross her hands humbly
As if praying dumbly,
Over her breast!

Owning her weakness,
Her evil behavior,
And leaving, with meekness,
Her sins to her Savior!

THIS is a thin poem: the word "thin" refers to the shortness of the lines which make the reading doubly difficult. You hardly set your course when the author brings you to a new line. Yet, the structure draws its strength from this arrangement of lines.

This is a poem of social protest. It could be adapted—and certainly had its parallels in the early 1930's—to any time of social stress when the creative people cry out against injustice. Is Hood a predecessor of Clifford Odets?

Because of the manner in which the poem is set up typographically, the reader will have to glue the thoughts together in his reading. Psychologically, the placement of words and the manner of punctuation affect the reading of any work. This particular grouping tempts the reader to use short and staccato phrasing. While there is an economy of words, it is just such economy that characterizes the mood. This poem is an editorial sketch rather than a detailed painting. Hood draws in the rough outlines to point up his horror at the kind of words that made the scene possible.

Read this poem as though you were on the spot holding the limp body in your arms. You are the attorney for the defense. The start is paced with slowness and mixed with sadness. In the ninth stanza the attorney rails against the society which committed the murder. It's here that the poem picks up speed, and a touch of bitterness and anger. Hold it down, or over-emotionalism would spoil the over-all effect. In the fourteenth stanza, revert to the pace and mood of the opening stanzas. Finish quietly. This is a poem that sets out to deliver a message by way of a story. It succeeds with quiet intensity and sadness, rather than by arm waving and full voicing. When you shout at somebody he usually shouts back, particularly if he feels a twinge of guilt. But when the rebuke is made quietly, the response is hard—and the effect is deep.

THE BATTLE OF BLENHEIM
Robert Southey

It was a summer's evening,
    Old Kaspar's work was done,
And he before his cottage door
    Was sitting in the sun;
And by him sported on the green
His little grandchild Wilhelmine.

She saw her brother Peterkin
    Roll something large and round,
Which he beside the rivulet,
    In playing there, had found;
He came to ask what he had found
That was so large and smooth and round.

Old Kaspar took it from the boy,
    Who stood expectant by;
And then the old man shook his head,
    And, with a natural sigh,
" 'Tis some poor fellow's skull," said he,
"Who fell in the great victory.

"I find them in the garden,
  For there's many hereabout;
And often, when I go to plough,
  The ploughshare turns them out;
For many thousand men," said he,
  "Were slain in the great victory."

"Now tell us what 'twas all about,"
  Young Peterkin he cries;
And little Wilhelmine looks up
  With wonder-waiting eyes;
"Now tell us all about the war,
And what they fought each other for."

"It was the English," Kaspar cried,
  "Who put the French to rout;
But what they fought each other for
  I could not well make out;
But everybody said," quoth he,
  "That 'twas a famous victory.

"My father lived at Blenheim then,
  Yon little stream hard by;
They burnt his dwelling to the ground,
  And he was forced to fly;
So with his wife and child he fled,
Nor had he where to rest his head.

"With fire and sword the country round
    Was wasted far and wide;
And many a childing mother there,
    And new-born baby died;
But things like that, you know, must be
At every famous victory.

"They say it was a shocking sight
    After the field was won,
For many thousand bodies here
    Lay rotting in the sun;
But things like that, you know, must be
After a famous victory.

"Great praise the Duke of Marlborough won,
    And our good Prince Eugene."
"Why, 'twas a very wicked thing!"
    Said little Wilhelmine.
"Nay, nay, my little girl!" quoth he,
"It was a famous victory.

"And everybody praised the Duke
    Who this great fight did win."
"But what good came of it at last?"
    Quoth little Peterkin.
"Why, that I cannot tell," said he;
"But 'twas a famous victory."

Perhaps the best refutation of the George Bernard Shaw epigram, "Youth is such a wonderful thing, it's a pity it's wasted on children," is expressed in this work.

For it is the two youngsters in the poem who make the sense. It is around them that the poem revolves. This is a poem about a battle, yet in the reading it becomes a strong sermon for peace. The old man, Kaspar, lives by opinions from a history book published out of perspective. He admits that dead men are a necessary by-product of a battle, but refuses to question whether the battle itself was necessary. It is the inquiring, naive questions of the two grandchildren who shake his convictions. They *do* teach the old dog a new trick. With their undistorted logic and under their cross-examination, they shake Kaspar into a realization that the monuments of memorial are intended as a tribute to men who died and not as an excuse for war.

At the beginning of the poem, Kaspar is sure of himself. For years he has quoted, " 'twas a famous victory." He has forgotten what the fight was about but took pride in the act of winning. He admits that his house was burned, that he and his family were left homeless, that other children had had their lives dismembered. "But things like that, you know, must be at every famous victory," he has decided.

At first, he draws on the reservoir of the countryside's cliché of pride in the triumph as an alibi for destruction. But when the tenth stanza comes around and Little Wilhelmine, after digesting the evidence, cries out that it was wicked, the old man pauses. Then the second volley is fired by little Peter, who questions, "But what good came of it at last?" Kaspar is left without an answer. He can only parrot himself and the broken-record of history and repeat that it was a famous victory.

By giving to Kaspar's lines a great conviction based on blind acceptance in the early part of the poem, you build him up for his fall. In the tenth stanza, he is not so sure of himself. In the eleventh, Peterkin scores a knockout; Kaspar is no longer certain. Don't let the words fool you. It is the reading of the last line that spices this poem and makes it a peace offering rather than a war memorial.

This effect can be created in two ways. First, by reading the lines slower than before, by treating them as though he were in daze, unsure of himself. Second, by making the last line a question. The word "victory," if inflected as a question, socks home a powerful peace idea. Try it.

In characterizing the leading players in the poem, give the weight and slowness of old age to Kaspar, the lightness and quickness of youth to the two children. Symbolically, Kaspar represents the old guard of conservatism and the two children, the advance guard of progressive thinking. More childlike—and the word is not used for chronological purposes—insistence of getting the facts will work for the days of peace.

CURFEW MUST NOT RING TONIGHT

Rosa Hartwick Thorpe

England's sun was slowly setting
O'er the hills so far away,
Filling all the land with beauty
At the close of one sad day;
And the last rays kissed the forehead
Of a man and maiden fair—
He with a step so slow and weakened,
She with sunny, floating hair;
He with sad bowed head, and thoughtful,
She with lips so cold and white,
Struggling to keep back the murmur,
"Curfew must not ring tonight."

"Sexton," Bessie's white lips faltered,
Pointing to the prison old,
With its walls so dark and gloomy—
Walls so dark, and damp, and cold—
"I've a lover in that prison,
Doomed this very night to die,
At the ringing of the curfew,
And no earthly help is nigh.
Cromwell will not come till sunset";
And her face grew strangely white,
As she spoke in husky whispers,
"Curfew must not ring tonight."

"Bessie," calmly spoke the sexton—
Every word pierced her young heart
Like a thousand gleaming arrows,
Like a deadly poisoned dart—
"Long, long years I've rung the curfew
From that gloomy shadowed tow'r;
Every evening, just at sunset,
It has told the twilight hour.
I have done my duty ever.
Tried to do it just and right;
Now I'm old, I will not miss it;
Girl, the curfew rings tonight!"

Wild her eyes and pale her features,
Stern and white her thoughtful brow,
And within her heart's deep center,
Bessie made a solemn vow.
She had listened while the judges
Read, without a tear or sigh,
"At the ringing of the curfew
Basil Underwood must die."
And her breath came fast and faster,
And her eyes grew large and bright;
One low murmur, scarcely spoken—
"Curfew must not ring tonight."

She with light step bounded forward,
Sprang within the old church door,
Left the old man coming slowly,
Paths he'd often trod before;
Not one moment paused the maiden,
But with cheek and brow aglow,
Staggered up the gloomy tower,
Where the bell swung to and fro;
Then she climbed the slimy ladder,
Dark, without one ray of light,
Upward still, her pale lips saying,
"Curfew shall not ring tonight."

She has reached the topmost ladder,
O'er her hangs the great dark bell,
And the awful gloom beneath her,
Like the pathway down to Hell.
See, the ponderous tongue is swinging,
'Tis the hour of curfew now;
And the sight has chilled her bosom,
Stopped her breath, and paled her brow.
Shall she let it ring? No, never!
Her eyes flash with sudden light,
As she springs and grasps it firmly—
"Curfew shall not ring tonight."

Out she swung, far out, the city
Seemed a tiny speck below;
There twixt heaven and earth suspended,
As the bell swung to and fro;
And the half-deaf sexton ringing
(Years he had not heard the bell)
And he thought the twilight curfew
Rang young Basil's funeral knell;
Still the maiden clinging firmly,
Cheek and brow so pale and white,
Stilled her frightened heart's wild beating—
"Curfew shall not ring tonight."

It was o'er—the bell ceased swaying,
And the maiden stepped once more
Firmly on the damp old ladder,
Where for hundred years before
Human foot had not been planted;
And what she this night had done
Should be told in long years after:
As the rays of setting sun
Light the sky with mellow beauty,
Aged sires with heads of white,
Tell the children why the curfew
Did not ring that one sad night.

O'er the distant hills came Cromwell;
Bessie saw him, and her brow,
Lately white with sickening terror,
Glows with sudden beauty now.
At his feet she told her story,
Showed her hands all bruised and torn;
And her sweet young face so haggard,
With a look so sad and worn,
Touched his heart with sudden pity,
Lit his eyes with misty light;
"Go, your lover lives!" cried Cromwell;
"Curfew shall not ring tonight."

I WOULD hardly want to read this one in front of an audience perfumed with sophistication. For one thing, Basil Underwood, the hero who stands to die at Curfew, somehow sounds like an alias of Groucho Marx. And the picture of the heroine, Bessie, holding on to the tongue of the bell is even more appropriate to the Penny Arcade than the ten, twent', thirt' theatre. One needs only to repeat a casual observation that this is one of the first printed documentations of a woman who held her tongue. The inevitable comparison calls up Pearl White in *The Perils of Pauline*. Today's funnybone activator was yesterday's heart accelerator. So let's treat Bessie as a period piece, not to be taken too seriously. Actually, any sexton who couldn't hear the bell ring could hardly have turned a deaf ear on the young lady's beseeching pleas to avoid his routined duty. Despite these contradictions, Bessie and Basil rate a place in this volume, for the sake of the record and the sneers of the sophisticates. It is perhaps as a yardstick of contrast that this poem has inched into this collection.

Not having the heart to detail an interpretation of this piece, I give to you "Curfew Must Not Ring Tonight" as a piece of mellydramer, as a showpiece for a masquerade party when you decide to come dressed up as a silo and are called on to perform. Treat this reading broadly. Play it for laughs.

CASABIANCA

Felicia Dorothea Hemans

In the battle of the Nile, thirteen-year-old Casabianca, son of the Admiral of the Orient, remained at his post after the ship had taken fire and all the guns had been abandoned. He perished when the vessel exploded.

The boy stood on the burning deck,
Whence all but he had fled;
The flame that lit the battle's wreck,
Shone round him o'er the dead.

Yet beautiful and bright he stood,
As born to rule the storm;
A creature of heroic blood,
A proud though childlike form.

The flames rolled on; he would not go
Without his father's word;
That father, faint in death below,
His voice no longer heard.

He called aloud, "Say, Father, say,
If yet my task is done!"
He knew not that the chieftain lay
Unconscious of his son.

"Speak, Father!" once again he cried,
"If I may yet be gone!"
—And but the booming shots replied,
And fast the flames rolled on.

Upon his brow he felt their breath,
And in his waving hair;
And looked from that lone post of death
In still yet brave despair;

And shouted but once more aloud,
"My Father! must I stay?"
While o'er him fast, through sail and shroud,
The wreathing fires made way.

They wrapt the ship in splendor wild,
They caught the flag on high,
And streamed above the gallant child,
Like banners in the sky.

There came a burst of thunder sound;
The boy—Oh! where was *he?*
—Ask of the winds, that far around
With fragments strewed the sea;—

With shroud, and mast, and pennon fair,
That well had borne their part,—
But the noblest thing that perished there
Was that young, faithful heart.

THIS is a sort of tabloid edition of poetry. It is a news story. In this piece Miss Hemans is a sob sister. Yet like most tabloid tear-jerkers, this poem has mass appeal and appears on the playbills of countless local classnights for junior Laurence Olivier's to display their dramatic talents. But set aside the reputation of this poem, and start afresh. Don't lead it out as warhorse to the pasture, but saddle it as though it were a young colt.

The boy who stood on the burning deck, when treated as an object of sorrow instead of being manhandled as an object of ridicule, comes alive in the hands of a skillful interpreter. Actually, its reputation rests on its first line and few have read it through to the end. In this respect the poem falls into the same clutches as "Woodman Spare That Tree."

Don't declaim this one. This is no place for heroic gestures. Start right off to send tradition into coventry. Break the rhythm in the first line; pause after "boy." In the third line, pause after "flame." This is a poem of action. Yet you will sink with the fleet if you fall into the trap of reading this poem *as* the boy. Rather read it as a reporter sending in a dispatch to your paper.

THE CHARGE OF THE LIGHT BRIGADE

Alfred, Lord Tennyson

Half a league, half a league,
Half a league onward,
All in the valley of Death
  Rode the six hundred.
  "Forward, the Light Brigade!
Charge for the guns!" he said.
Into the valley of Death
  Rode the six hundred.

"Forward, the Light Brigade!"
Was there a man dismayed?
Not though the soldier knew
  Some one had blundered.
Theirs not to make reply,
Theirs not to reason why,
Theirs but to do and die.
Into the valley of Death
  Rode the six hundred.

Cannon to right of them,
Cannon to left of them,
Cannon in front of them
  Volleyed and thundered;

Stormed at with shot and shell,
Boldly they rode and well,
Into the jaws of Death,
Into the mouth of Hell
   Rode the six hundred.

Flashed all their sabres bare,
Flashed as they turned in air
Sabring the gunners there,
Charging an army, while
   All the world wondered:
Plunged in the battery-smoke
Right through the line they broke;
Cossack and Russian
Reeled from the sabre-stroke
   Shattered and sundered.
Then they rode back, but not,
   Not the six hundred.

Cannon to right of them,
Cannon to left of them,
Cannon behind them
   Volleyed and thundered;
Stormed at with shot and shell,
While horse and hero fell,
They that had fought so well

Came through the jaws of Death,
Back from the mouth of Hell,
All that was left of them,
  Left of six hundred.

When can their glory fade?
O the wild charge they made!
  All the world wondered.
Honor the charge they made!
Honor the Light Brigade,
  Noble six hundred!

THE words of this poem leap off the page and onto the tongue of the reader. It is an action piece loaded with the gunpowder of excitement. The level-headed and the peace fighters will ponder whether this poem isn't a shot of militaristic adrenalin. This work is like the music of a military band. No matter how you feel it steps up the tempo of your heart beats. We do not include this poem for its moral values, but rather as a demonstration of its ability to stir the emotions . . . also to suggest that war-less lifetimes can be won by getting people as excited about peace as they get about war. Peace, like war, calls for poetry of action. Too often is peace considered the inactive state of man. We need the poets to drum up the excitement of peace instead of settling down into the sedative of pastoral scenes.

The pace of this reading is brisk. It is action throughout. Here the stoop-shouldered citizen puts on his uniform, straightens up, thrusts out his chest, snaps to attention. In the fourth stanza, the break comes after the tenth line. One stops abruptly, like a broken-field runner on a football gridiron who changes direction to avoid being tackled. Slow up on these two lines. The pace keeps its slow tempo. Note that the pattern first found in the third stanza is repeated here in the fifth. The change of the words from "in front of" to "behind" indicates the waning of the battle and the excitement. In the last two lines of this stanza note the use of the word "left." The second time hold the word "left" and take a pause before continuing; it is a word description of the casualty lists. In the last stanza, emphasize and pause after both uses of the word "honor."

THE FOOL'S PRAYER

Edward Rowland Sill

The royal feast was done; the King
Sought some new sport to banish care,
And to his jester cried: "Sir Fool,
Kneel now, and make for us a prayer!"

The jester doffed his cap and bells,
And stood the mocking court before;
They could not see the bitter smile
Behind the painted grin he wore.

He bowed his head, and bent his knee
Upon the monarch's silken stool;
His pleading voice arose: "O Lord,
Be merciful to me, a fool!

"No pity, Lord, could change the heart
From red with wrong to white as wool;
The rod must heal the sin; but, Lord,
Be merciful to me, a fool!

" 'Tis not by guilt, the onward sweep
Of truth and right, O Lord, we stay;
'Tis by our follies that so long
We hold the earth from heaven away.

"These clumsy feet, still in the mire,
Go crushing blossoms without end;
These hard, well-meaning hands we thrust
Among the heart-strings of a friend.

"The ill-timed truth we might have kept—
Who knows how sharp it pierced and stung!
The words we had not sense to say—
Who knows how grandly it had rung!

"Our faults no tenderness should ask,
The chastening strips must cleanse them all;
But for our blunders—oh, in shame
Before the eyes of heaven we fall.

"Earth bears no balsam for mistakes;
Men crown the knave, and scourge the tool
That did his will; but Thou, O Lord,
Be merciful to me, a fool!"

The room was hushed; in silence rose
The King, and sought his gardens cool,
And walked apart, and murmured low,
"Be merciful to me, a fool!"

In Richard II, poet Shakespeare wrote:

> For within the hollow crown
> That rounds the mortal temples of a king
> Keeps Death his court; and there the antic sits,
> Scoffing his state, and grinning at his pomp;
> Allowing him a breath, a little scene,
> To monarchize, be fear'd, and kill with looks;
> Infusing him with self and vain conceit,
> As if this flesh, which walls about our life,
> Were brass impregnable; and humour'd thus,
> Comes at the last, and with a little pin
> Bores through his castle-wall, and—farewell, king!

Here is a documentation of that philosophy. This is a religious poem. It re-establishes the power of God over mortal kings; replaces the king's crown with the fool's cap of his jester. It slaps down the earthly king who mistook his ermine for a halo.

When the King mockingly calls his jester "Sir" and commands him to make a prayer, he is challenging not only the humorous ability of his slave, but the might of God, Himself. It is through the prayer of the Fool that God rebukes the King and sends him into his garden, with its natural surroundings, to knight himself with the nomenclature of a slave.

The first stanza sets the scene. This is the background; the reader matches it with his manner. The King's lines must be characterized. It is even logical to put in an unwritten laugh after the fourth line. The impact of the poem derives from the position of the Fool at the foot of the throne. The King and his court must surely at first believe that the Jester is

praying to him. This effect can be achieved by reading the
Jester's lines with a slight touch of characterization labelling
him in his role as jester. But easily and quickly his voice gets
richer, deeper, his lines are read with more sincerity. The fool
is gone and the penitent takes his place. In the ninth stanza,
the poem reaches its vocal climax; the moral climax is reserved for the last line of the poem.

The last stanza is difficult to do properly. Its success
hinges directly on the reading of the last line of the ninth
stanza. Here the Jester verges on teardom. Pause after "merciful to me" and read "a fool" with finality. In the last line
of the poem, the King repeats the words of his Jester. He, too,
is shaken—perhaps more so. But the Jester has made his confession and the King remains suspended between sin and hope
for forgiveness, sure of the first, but uncertain of the latter.
Read the words "a fool" in this last line without resolving the
line, keeping the sound suspended. This is very much like an
unresolved chord played on the piano. Also, in this line emphasize "me." The real fool has been identified!

OLD IRONSIDES

Oliver Wendell Holmes

Ay, tear her tattered ensign down!
  Long has it waved on high,
And many an eye has danced to see
  That banner in the sky;
Beneath it rung the battle shout,
  And burst the cannon's roar;—
The meteor of the ocean air
  Shall sweep the clouds no more.

Her deck, once red with heroes' blood,
  Where knelt the vanquished foe,
When winds were hurrying o'er the flood,
  And waves were white below,
No more shall feel the victor's tread,
  Or know the conquered knee;—
The harpies of the shore shall pluck
  The eagle of the sea!

Oh, better that her shattered hulk
Should sink beneath the wave;
Her thunders shook the mighty deep,
And there should be her grave;
Nail to the mast her holy flag,
Set every threadbare sail,
And give her to the god of storms,
The lightning and the gale!

WHEN the news arrived that Congress had decided to sink the battle-scarred and time-honored ship, "Old Ironsides," the sentimentalists and the patriots protested. This poem is the most effective of those protests. The usual politicians' thunder rolling polysyllabically up and down the halls of Congress is weak and watered compared to Oliver Wendell Holmes' under-playing.

"Methinks the gentleman doth protest too much" would have been a sure answer to a repetitious set of complaints. So, instead, Holmes has used the effective psychology of reversing the complaint: "You want to get rid of Old Ironsides? Go ahead!" In effect, he is adopting the same position as a man who is about to be fired after years of service. He doesn't shout, "You can't do this to me!" Instead he say, "All right. If that's the way you want it. I got that big order from the Randall Company. I took a cut when business was bad. I watched the company, while you were sick in the hospital, as though it were my own. You told me *then* you'd never forget it. Very well. Now you want to fire me. All right. If that's the way you want it."

In the first manner, he would have had a yelling contest with the employer. By the second approach, he shames him. This is the tack that Holmes took. "All right," he says, "Tear her tattered ensign down!" It is by reminding the country, in the guise of agreement, of Old Ironsides' past that he insures its future.

P.S., the ship was saved!

GOD'S-ACRE

Henry Wadsworth Longfellow

I like that ancient Saxon phrase, which calls
　The burial-ground God's-Acre! It is just;
It consecrates each grave within its walls,
　And breathes a benison o'er the sleeping dust.

God's-Acre! Yes, that blessed name imparts
　Comfort to those who in the grave have sown
The seed that they had garnered in their hearts,
　Their bread of life, alas! no more their own.

Into its furrows shall we all be cast,
　In the sure faith, that we shall rise again
At the great harvest, when the archangel's blast
　Shall winnow, like a fan, the chaff and grain.

Then shall the good stand in immortal bloom,
　In the fair garden of that second birth;
And each bright blossom mingle its perfume
　With that of flowers, which never bloomed on ear

With thy rude plowshare, Death, turn up the sod,
　And spread the furrow for the seed we sow;
This is the field and Acre of our God,
　This is the place where human harvests grow.

THIS is a very comforting poem as the funeral service is a comfort to those who remain behind; its simple imagery deserves an honored place on the arches of our cemeteries. This poem helps turn loss into profit on the balance sheet of existence. Unlike so many promises of the Hereafter, it is told with simplicity. It is almost matter of fact. By tying the unknown to the known, Longfellow manages to take some of the mystery out of death.

A simple reading is best. No dramatics; no tears. Before you start the actual reading of the poem, picture yourself smoking a pipe and saying to a friend, "You know something . . ." Then start reading.

In the second line, pause after "burial-ground." "God's-Acre" must stand by itself as a continuing motive throughout the piece. When you strike that word again in the second stanza, underline "God's" both by emphasis and by a slight pause after saying it. In this stanza, take your breath after "grave." In the fourth stanza, underline "Then." In the fifth, treat the last two lines as definite statements apart from the rest. In each, underline the word "This."

THE WRECK OF THE HESPERUS

Henry Wadsworth Longfellow

It was the schooner Hesperus,
That sailed the wintry sea;
And the skipper had taken his little daughter,
To bear him company.

Blue were her eyes as the fairy flax,
Her cheeks like the dawn of day,
And her bosom white as the hawthorn buds
That ope in the month of May.

The skipper he stood beside the helm,
His pipe was in his mouth,
And he watched how the veering flaw did blow
The smoke now West, now South.

Then up and spake an old Sailor,
Had sailed to the Spanish Main,
"I pray thee, put into yonder port,
For I fear a hurricane.

"Last night, the moon had a golden ring,
And to-night no moon we see!"
The skipper, he blew a whiff from his pipe,
And a scornful laugh laughed he.

Colder and colder blew the wind,
A gale from the Northeast;
The snow fell hissing in the brine,
And the billows frothed like yeast.

Down came the storm, and smote amain
The vessel in its strength;
She shuddered and paused, like a frightened steed,
Then leaped her cable's length.

"Come hither! come hither! my little daughter,
And do not tremble so;
For I can weather the roughest gale
That ever wind did blow."

He wrapped her warm in his seaman's coat
Against the stinging blast;
He cut a rope from a broken spar,
And bound her to the mast.

"O father! I hear the church-bells ring,
Oh say, what may it be?"
" 'Tis a fog-bell on a rock-bound coast!"
And he steered for the open sea.

"O father! I hear the sound of guns,
Oh say, what may it be?"
"Some ship in distress, that cannot live
In such an angry sea!"

"O father! I see a gleaming light,
Oh say, what may it be?"
But the father answered never a word,
A frozen corpse was he.

Lashed to the helm, all stiff and stark,
With his face turned to the skies,
The lantern gleamed through the gleaming snow
On his fixed and glassy eyes.

Then the maiden clasped her hands and prayed
That saved she might be;
And she thought of Christ, who stilled the waves
On the Lake of Galilee.

And fast through the midnight dark and drear,
Through the whistling sleet and snow,
Like a sheeted ghost, the vessel swept
Towards the reef of Norman's Woe.

And ever the fitful gusts between
A sound came from the land;
It was the sound of trampling surf,
On the rocks and the hard sea-sand.

The breakers were right beneath her bows,
She drifted a dreary wreck,
And a whooping billow swept the crew
Like icicles from her deck.

She struck where the white and fleecy waves
Looked soft as carded wool,
But the cruel rocks, they gored her side
Like the horns of an angry bull.

Her rattling shrouds, all sheathed in ice,
With the masts went by the board;
Like a vessel of glass, she stove and sank,
Ho! Ho! the breakers roared!

At daybreak, on the bleak sea-beach,
A fisherman stood aghast,
To see the form of a maiden fair,
Lashed close to a drifting mast!

The salt sea was frozen on her breast,
The salt tears in her eyes;
And he saw her hair, like the brown sea-weed,
On the billows fall and rise.

Such was the wreck of the Hesperus,
In the midnight and the snow!
Christ save us all from a death like this,
On the reef of Norman's Woe!

THIS poem has all the elements (and battles most of them) to make what frequently becomes "An Old Favorite." It has a storm, a lovely little girl, the inevitability of tragedy, a hard-minded father, and that most dashing of all battles—a fight beween man and nature.

As "An Old Favorite" it has fought the storms of many Amateur Elocutionists who tried to steer it into the port of Audience Applause. It *is* an effective piece. By avoiding a florid and heroic rendition, and exercising restraint, you can save this one from the Davy Jones locker of hackneyed pieces. This poem does not call for a "gra-a-nd" manner of delivery. As an overture to our reading suggestions, may we urge that the first line not be read in one lump; rather, emphasize the word "It" instead of underlining (as is usually done) the word "was."

The first stanza is scene setting. The ship is going along smoothly. In the second, if this were a movie script, the camera would "pan" to a closeup of the little girl. Here we need a soft reading to match the prettiness of the child; but don't get too saccharine. In the third, we switch to a closeup of the Captain; match his personality—he is strong, rough. Then, in the third stanza, the action starts to build. The Sailor is respect-ful but urgent. In the fifth stanza, switch on the third line from the respectful quality of the sailor to the strong, assured roughness of the Captain. Now start to build tonally. The sixth and seventh stanzas are full of sound and fury. The eighth still moving along, but don't try to shout above the storm sounds you just created. Achieve your effects by increasing tempo rather than volume. In the following stanzas build up the girl's questioning; but start low enough to give yourself a chance to go up the ladder of excitement. In the twelfth stanza, the questions have reached their highest pitch of intensity. After the second line, pause; make it a good long pause. Read the next two lines slowly and grimly.

The next stanza is a memorial service read over the dead Captain. Try for depth and resonance. Give it a measured reading.

Now start to build again—but gradually, not all at once. Build through the eighteenth stanza. This is the highest point in his sequence of action.

Then pause. Count four slowly. Then, begin again. The closing three paragraphs call for a slow reading. The very last one personalizes the poem. While it is part of the poem, it is apart from the action. It is a prayer. Read it even more slowly and more quietly than any other part of the work.

INCIDENT OF THE FRENCH CAMP

Robert Browning

You know, we French stormed Ratisbon:
    A mile or so away,
On a little mound, Napoleon
    Stood on our storming-day;
With neck out-thrust, you fancy how,
    Legs wide, arms locked behind,
As if to balance the prone brow
    Oppressive with its mind.

Just as perhaps he mused, "My plans
    That soar, to earth may fall,
Let once my army-leader Lannes
    Waver at yonder wall,"—
Out 'twixt the battery-smokes there flew
    A rider, bound on bound
Full-galloping; nor bridle drew
    Until he reached the mound.

Then off there flung in smiling joy,
    And held himself erect

By just his horse's mane, a boy:
    You hardly could suspect—
(So tight he kept his lips compressed,
    Scarce any blood came through),
You looked twice ere you saw his breast
    Was all but shot in two.

"Well," cried he, "Emperor, by God's grace
    We've got you Ratisbon!
The Marshal's in the market-place,
    And you'll be there anon
To see your flag-bird flap his vans
    Where I, to heart's desire,
Perched him!" The chief's eye flashed; his plans
    Soared up again like fire.

The chief's eye flashed; but presently
    Softened itself, as sheathes
A film the mother-eagle's eye
    When her bruised eaglet breathes;
"You're wounded!" "Nay," the soldier's pride
    Touched to the quick, he said:
"I'm killed, Sire!" And his chief beside,
    Smiling, the boy fell dead.

H ERE is a poetic communiqué from Napoleon's head-quarters, a versified Croix de Guerre, posthumously awarded. Like all citations, it is told from the perspective of the narrator.

To set the scene, place yourself in a bar-room frequented by soldiers. The drinks have been passed around, and each soldier is boasting of the feats of his regiment. It is now your turn and you tell the story of the Messenger and the Marshall. The poem opens narratively. The descriptions are slides in a projector, you switch from one to the other, and each is brought out as a highlight. The first stanza will therefore have to be read like the parts of a prefabricated house, each in itself performing a function to the end of solidifying the whole. The first line is almost a paragraph by itself. Underline the words "stood," "out-thrust," "wide," "locked behind"; these are descriptions and emphasizing them sketches in the picture you are drawing.

In the second stanza, treat the word "just" as an action word. It is as though the forward motion of the piece begins at this point. In the fourth stanza, the action is heroic; the quotations are full of fire. Carry this pace through to the speech "I'm killed, Sire!" Then pause and softly read the poem to conclusion.

This piece derives its excitement not from a fast movement of the action but from the intensity of the situation itself. It is a boastful poem, boldly colored by the pride of nationalism. To the reader, Browning poses a problem. He generates the excitement by rolling words together almost in contempt of the problem of finding places to get new breaths to continue. But that is a clue to a successful rendition; this is a breathless work. Take the lines in the second stanza: "Out 'twixt the battery-smokes there flew a rider, bound on bound full galloping; nor bridle drew until he reached the mound." That's quite a distance to race on one breath. But it can be done with practice. It also commands the reader to use not too much volume but to carry this action along in the manner of a story teller, rather than in the ringing tones of an actor. That is why, specifically, at the start of this annotation, we set the scene in a gathering of soldiers and emphasized the fact that this is told from the perspective of the narrator.

THE LEAK IN THE DIKE

Phoebe Cary

The good dame looked from her cottage
    At the close of the pleasant day,
And cheerily called to her little son
    Outside the door at play:
"Come, Peter! come! I want you to go,
    While there is light to see,
To the hut of the blind old man who lives
    Across the dike, for me;
And take these cakes I made for him—
    They are hot and smoking yet;
You have time enough to go and come
    Before the sun is set."

Then the good wife turned to her labor,
    Humming a simple song,
And thought of her husband working hard
    At the sluices all day long;
And set the turf a-blazing,
    And brought the coarse black bread:
That he might find a fire at night,
    And find the table spread.

And Peter left the brother,
    With whom all day he had played,

And the sister who had watched their sports
In the willow's tender shade;
And told them they'd see him back before
They saw a star in sight,
Though he wouldn't be afraid to go
In the very darkest night!
For he was a brave, bright fellow,
With eye and conscience clear;
He could do whatever a boy might do,
And he had not learned to fear.
Why, he wouldn't have robbed a bird's nest,
Nor brought a stork to harm,
Though never a law in Holland
Had stood to stay his arm!

And now with his face all glowing,
And eyes as bright as the day
With the thoughts of his pleasant errand,
He trudged along the way;
And soon his joyous prattle
Made glad a lonesome place—
Alas! if only the blind old man
Could have seen that happy face!
Yet he somehow caught the brightness
Which his voice and presence lent
And he felt the sunshine come and go
As Peter came and went.

And now, as the day was sinking,
  And the winds began to rise,
The mother looked from her door again,
  Shading her anxious eyes,
And saw the shadows deepen
  And birds to their home come back,
But never a sign of Peter
  Along the level track.
But she said: "He will come at morning,
  So I need not fret or grieve—
Though it isn't like my boy at all
  To stay without my leave."

But where was the child delaying?
  On the homeward way was he,
And across the dike while the sun was up
  An hour above the sea.
He was stopping now to gather flowers,
  Now listening to the sound,
As the angry waters dashed themselves
  Against their narrow bound.
"Ah! well for us," said Peter,
  "That the gates are good and strong,
And my father tends them carefully,
  Or they would not hold you long!

You're a wicked sea," said Peter;
"I know why you fret and chafe;
You would like to spoil our lands and homes;
But our sluices keep you safe."

But hark! through the noise of waters
Comes a low, clear, trickling sound;
And the child's face pales with terror,
And his blossoms drop to the ground.
He is up the bank in a moment,
And, stealing through the sand,
He sees a stream not yet so large
As his slender, childish hand.

'Tis a leak in the dike!—He is but a boy,
Unused to fearful scenes;
But, young as he is, he has learned to know
The dreadful thing that means.
A leak in the dike! The stoutest heart
Grows faint that cry to hear,
And the bravest man in all the land
Turns white with mortal fear.
For he knows the smallest leak may grow
To a flood in a single night;
And he knows the strength of the cruel sea
When loosed in its angry might.

And the Boy! he has seen the danger
  And, shouting a wild alarm,
He forces back the weight of the sea
  With the strength of his single arm!
He listens for the joyful sound
  Of a footstep passing nigh;
And lays his ear to the ground, to catch
  The answer to his cry.
And he hears the rough winds blowing,
  And the waters rise and fall,
But never an answer comes to him
  Save the echo of his call.
He sees no hope, no succor,
  His feeble voice is lost;
Yet what shall he do but watch and wait
  Though he perish at his post!

So, faintly calling and crying
  Till the sun is under the sea;
Crying and moaning till the stars
  Come out for company;
He thinks of his brother and sister,
  Asleep in their safe warm bed;
He thinks of his father and mother,
  Of himself as dying—and dead;

And of how, when the night is over,
    They must come and find him at last;
But he never thinks he can leave the place
    Where duty holds him fast.

The good dame in the cottage
    Is up and astir with the light,
For the thought of her little Peter
    Has been with her all night.
And now she watches the pathway,
    As yester-eve she had done;
But what does she see so strange and black
    Against the rising sun?
Her neighbors are bearing between them
    Something straight to her door;
Her child is coming home, but not
    As he ever came before!

"He is dead!" she cries, "my darling!"
    And the startled father hears,
And comes and looks the way she looks,
    And fears the things she fears;
Till a glad shout from the bearers
    Thrills the stricken man and wife—

"Give thanks, for your son has saved our land,
    And God has saved his life!"
So, there in the morning sunshine
    They knelt about the boy;
And every head was bared and bent
    In tearful, reverent joy.

'Tis many a year since then; but still,
    When the sea roars like a flood,
The boys are taught what a boy can do
    Who is brave and true and good;
For every man in that country
    Takes his son by the hand
And tells him of little Peter,
    Whose courage saved the land.

They have many a valiant hero,
    Remembered through the years;
But never one whose name so oft
    Is named with loving tears.
And his deed shall be sung by the cradle,
    And told to the child on the knee,
So long as the dikes of Holland
    Divide the land from the sea!

THERE are certain stories that belong on the bookshelf of every child. "The Leak in the Dike" is one of these and consequently belongs in the repertory of Gesell-following fathers.

This poem is a sort of male version of *Little Red Riding Hood:* the mother sends her child with a package for an infirm old man (the grandmother). On the way, he meets a problem (the wolf). But here male action supersedes womanly susceptibility to temptation; the young boy needs no woodchopper to help him out of his mess. Fathers will find this easier to recite to youngsters than *Little Red Riding Hood,* who had practically no worthy characteristics of any kind. Besides, it will be less trouble than explaining how the wolf could eat the grandmother who nevertheless remains alive as the curtain falls. Your major explanation will be in describing a dike, which calls more for facts than fancies.

Like all good children's stories, this one starts in the manner of "Once Upon a Time." The opening lines call for a relaxed reading, giving you enough time to work yourself into a lather of excitement. The fourth line starts the errand. While you will not want to effect a falsetto (you'll never convince your child that you're his mother) you should characterize the lines. Treat each four lines as a unit; this simple form of rhyme is dear to the ears of children and they respond to simple rhythms. Again the easy manner of reading, matching up the lines in units of four will bring out the rhythms of the piece.

In the third stanza, at the eighth line, it will be effective to mimic Peter's braggadocio. You can help this effect by pausing after "though." In the fourth stanza, pick up the pace a trifle as an overture to impending action. In the fifth stanza, let your voice deepen, and let a note of anxiety enter into it.

The question that tops off the sixth stanza is dramatic. Ask it; pause; and then read on for the answer is given at once. When you reach Peter's quotes, take on his characterization, talk up in the manner of a young boy who is sure of himself and perhaps slightly boastful. (You've heard the kind of tone a child uses when he tells the kid across the street, "My father can lick your father any day.")

At the seventh stanza, start picking up your pace. Note and follow the clue of the exclamation point after "hark!" Pause after this and then rush on. When you reach the italicized phrase " 'Tis a leak in the Dike" you will have to convey the implications of the situation—horror mixed with excitement! In the second line, emphasize the word "fearful." The second "Leak in the Dike" is not so big tonally as the first. Here, there is not the note of discovery but the note of danger; it is most easily expressed by a breathy voice, almost a whispering. Now the poem reaches its highest point of excitement. This carries through the ninth stanza.

Now soften your voice, move at a slower pace. In the eleventh stanza, when you reach the seventh line, set the scene for action. Break off after the word "but," pause, and then let your voice go up. In the eleventh line, the "but" gives an opportunity for a dramatic trick: Read it, "Her child is coming home, but" (pause—change tone to one of anxiety—then slowly) "but not . . . as . . . he . . . ever . . . came . . . before . . ." Now, a quick upsurge in the forward motion, carry the excitement along with a swifter pace.

In the twelfth stanza, there is a change of pace at the fifth line. The anxiety point has been passed and now the whole reading softens as though you are speaking a message to story over the soft roll of drums.

THE PUZZLED CENSUS TAKER

John Godfrey Saxe

"Got any boys?" the Marshal said
To a lady from over the Rhine;
And the lady shook her flaxen head,
And civilly answered, *"Nein!"*

"Got any girls?" the Marshal said
To the lady from over the Rhine;
And again the lady shook her head,
And civilly answered, *"Nein!"*

"But some are dead?" the Marshal said
To the lady from over the Rhine;
And again the lady shook her head,
And civilly answered, *"Nein!"*

"Husband of course?" the Marshal said
   To the lady from over the Rhine;
And again she shook her flaxen head,
   And civilly answered, *"Nein!"*

"The devil you have!" the Marshal said
   To the lady from over the Rhine;
And again she shook her flaxen head,
   And civilly answered, *"Nein!"*

"Now what do you mean by shaking your head,
   And always answering 'Nine'?"
"Ich kann nicht Englisch!" civilly said
   The lady from over the Rhine.

THERE is more pun here than poem. It achieves its point as spoken material in a fashion that is only hinted at by the written word. This is a fun piece and a puzzle to the listener though an obvious play on words to the reader. The pun, while it is obvious in the seeing, is explained to the listening audience only at that point where the woman speaks in German in the second line before the end. It is here that the auditor checks back over what he has heard and smiles his way through the poem in retrospect. This is no belly-laugh, but a work that is most easily pegged by the usually-abused word, "cute."

Like all farces, the fun comes from reading the poem "straight." One laugh—and the game is lost. It will help, too, to cheat a little. Read the word "Nein" each time it appears in the manner that a woman usually would answer if she really had nine children, nine husbands, etc. To heighten the impact of the closing stanza, we further suggest the deletion of the fifth stanza. It is the only one in which the "Nein" does not carry the same logic as the "Nine." We print it purely for the purists.

THE NIGHTINGALE AND THE GLOW-WORM

William Cowper

A Nightingale, that all day long
Had cheered the village with his song,
Nor yet at eve his note suspended,
Nor yet when eventide was ended,
Began to feel, as well he might,
The keen demands of appetite;
When, looking eagerly around,
He spied far off, upon the ground,
A something shining in the dark,
And knew the glow-worm by his spark;
So, stooping down from hawthorn top,
He thought to put him in his crop.
The worm, aware of his intent,
Harangued him thus, right eloquent:
"Did you admire my lamp," quoth he,
"As much as I your minstrelsy,
You would abhor to do me wrong,
As much as I to spoil your song;
For 'twas the self-same Power Divine
Taught you to sing, and me to shine;

That you with music, I with light,
Might beautify and cheer the night."
The songster heard his short oration,
And warbling out his approbation,
Released him, as my story tells,
And found a supper somewhere else.

    Hence jarring sectaries may learn
Their real interest to discern;
That brother should not war with brother,
And worry and devour each other;
But sing and shine by sweet consent,
Till life's poor transient night is spent,
Respecting in each other's case
The gifts of nature and of grace.
    Those Christians best deserve the name
Who studiously make peace their aim:
Peace both the duty and the prize
Of him that creeps and him that flies.

THE bird and the insect are the co-stars of an amusing comedy sketch, who, by the addition of the closing stanza, become the leading players in a fable. For this is a poem with a postscript. The reader has his choice (the precedent for this was suggested by certain anthologists) of stripping the poem of its postscript and treating it as a unit of comedy or following through the entire work and re-aligning his reading to make it a fable. Depending upon the choice, the interpretation has different values.

First, let's handle it as a comedy poem. The hungry Nightingale faces the cunning of the Worm in a situation reminiscent of the Aesop portrait of "The Lion and the Mouse." In this version, the Glow-worm must be characterized sharply; he is a slick super-salesman with all the legal cunning of Clarence Darrow. To make his point he combines eloquence with logic. When he gets through, we appreciate his ability at getting himself out of a tough spot. In this reading, the Glow-worm uses the Divine Power as a file to open the prison bars.

When the poem is read as a whole, the moral is serious enough to warrant an elimination of the broad characterization of the Worm. He sets up the point of the moral, and instead of someone beating a murder rap he becomes an evangelist. Ministers have long known that the congregation is more easily interested if it is given a dramatic situation before drawing on that situation to hit home with their spiritual lesson.

In either case, there is a delicious use of the word "something" in the ninth line. Hold up when you reach it. The author acts as though he is fishing around in his mind for the right word of description. He sees a . . . well, a . . . a something. It is a general word that couldn't be more specific or colorful.

Exercise care in the reading of the last stanza not to become too preachy. The moral is dictated by the preceding situation and it would be improper to get "grand" after the simplicity of the original set-up. Easy does it!

ODE
Arthur O'Shaughnessy

We are the music-makers,
  And we are the dreamers of dreams,
Wandering by lone sea-breakers,
  And sitting by desolate streams;
World-losers and world-forsakers,
  On whom the pale moon gleams:
Yet we are the movers and shakers
  Of the world for ever, it seems.

With wonderful deathless ditties
  We build up the world's great cities,
And out of a fabulous story
  We fashion an empire's glory:
One man with a dream, at pleasure,
  Shall go forth and conquer a crown;
And three with a new song's measure
  Can trample an empire down.

We, in the ages lying,
  In the buried past of the earth,
Built Nineveh with our sighing,
  And Babel itself with our mirth;
And o'erthrew them with prophesying
  To the old of the new world's worth;
For each age is a dream that is dying,
  Or one that is coming to birth.

THIS is the universal anthem of the propagandists. Note the distinction between musicians and music-makers, the difference between dreamers and dreamers of dreams. This poem salutes and commemorates the artist who is also a craftsman.

The long-curled poet is not the subject of this poem; the absent-minded professors of music are cancelled out. This is a militant piece, firm and full of resolution. These are teachers who became doers. This poem is a celebration and not an apology. Read it with energy.

In the last stanza, note the credit that is claimed in changing the world: "And o'erthrew them with prophesying to the old of the new world's worth." Put "new world" in capital letters—and you have a direction for the information sections of the United Nations. Each time "we" appears, underscore it and take a beat after saying it.

BARBARA FRIETCHIE
John Greenleaf Whittier

Up from the meadows rich with corn,
Clear in the cool September morn,
The clustered spires of Frederick stand
Green-walled by the hills of Maryland.

Round about them orchards sweep,
Apple and peach tree fruited deep,
Fair as the garden of the Lord
To the eyes of the famished rebel horde,
On that pleasant morn of the early fall
When Lee marched over the mountain-wall:
Over the mountains winding down,
Horse and foot, into Frederick town.

Forty flags with their silver stars,
Forty flags with their crimson bars,
Flapped in the morning wind: the sun
Of noon looked down, and saw not one.

Up rose old Barbara Frietchie then,
Bowed with her fourscore years and ten;
Bravest of all in Frederick town,
She took up the flag the men hauled down;
In her attic window the staff she set,
To show that one heart was loyal yet.

Up the street came the rebel tread,
Stonewall Jackson riding ahead.

Under his slouched hat left and right
He glanced; the old flag met his sight.

"Halt!"—the dust-brown ranks stood fast.
"Fire!"—out blazed the rifle-blast.

It shivered the window, pane and sash;
It rent the banner with seam and gash.

Quick as it fell, from the broken staff
Dame Barbara snatched the silken scarf.
She leaned far out on the window-sill,
And shook it forth with a royal will.
"Shoot, if you must, this old gray head,
But spare your country's flag," she said.

A shade of sadness, a blush of shame,
Over the face of the leader came;
The nobler nature whithin him stirred
To life at that woman's deed and word;
"Who touches a hair of yon gray head
Dies like a dog! March on!" he said.

All day long through Frederick street
Sounded the tread of marching feet:
All day long that free flag tossed
Over the heads of the rebel host.

Ever its torn folds rose and fell
On the loyal winds that loved it well;
And through the hill-gaps sunset light
Shone over it with a warm good-night.

Barbara Frietchie's work is o'er,
And the Rebel rides on his raids no more.

Honor to her! and let a tear
Fall, for her sake, on Stonewall's bier.

Over Barbara Frietchie's grave,
Flag of Freedom and Union, wave!

Peace and order and beauty draw
Round thy symbol of light and law;
And ever the stars above look down
On thy stars below in Frederick town!

W HITTIER'S penchant for two-line stanzas contributes a hazard for the reader of the spoken word. As in Whittier's other famous poem, "Maud Muller," the annotator has chosen (with explanation) to fuse some of the verses together to make the reading easier. White space between verses has a way of slowing the reader down like a red light, despite the need to follow the structure of the poem's action and pick up tempo. The symmetrical appearance of the printed word must occasionally give way to make a better road map for the one who is reading aloud.

Like all favorites, "Barbara Frietchie" has become a satirical canapé at the cocktail parties of the sophisticates. The line that cues their laughs is, of course, "Shoot, if you must, this old gray head." This is another of those cases where the jury returns a verdict of guilty on circumstantial evidence. Too many readers need to be anchored to the fact of Barbara's age. She is, after all, four score and ten; a ninety-year old woman 's scarcely characterized aptly by the usual bellowing manner of delivering this line.

It is hard to tell who the real hero of this poem is— Barbara Frietchie or Stonewall Jackson. Perhaps as a sedative to the feelings of the North and South, the game ends in a e score, with each contributing his share of humanity. Therere, don't slur away Jackson's contribution to the humanities the poem.

In moving into Barbara's famous speech, keep the pace oving along at the speed of the action, but the speech itself read slowly and quietly. In other words, keep up the pace the invasion, match it with Barbara's actions, but make speech believable by underplaying it.

ASK AND HAVE
Samuel Lover

"Oh, 'tis time I should talk to your mother,
Sweet Mary," says I;
"Oh, don't talk to my mother," says Mary,
Beginning to cry:
"For my mother says men are deceivers,
And never, I know, will consent;
She says girls in a hurry to marry,
At leisure repent."

"Then, suppose I would talk to your father,
Sweet Mary," says I;
"Oh, don't talk to my father," says Mary,
Beginning to cry:
"For my father he loves me so dearly,
He'll never consent I should go—
If you talk to my father," says Mary,
"He'll surely say, 'No.'"

"Then how shall I get you, my jewel?
Sweet Mary," says I;
"If your father and mother's so cruel,
Most surely I'll die!"
"Oh, never say die, dear," says Mary;
"A way now to save you I see;
Since my parents are both so contrary—
You'd better ask me!"

THERE is a rumor, as yet unconfirmed, that members of the female sex (a phrase used to distinguish them from "women") are able to turn on and off their tears in a manner that is almost electronic in its mechanism and supersonic in its speed. Witness the case of the young lady who co-stars in the above episode. It is her specific ability to turn on the waterworks that lends this poem its interest.

Take care in your characterization of her to give a weeping *effect* rather than produce the tears themselves. *Suggesting* an emotion is a more effective method of getting the auditor to respond than actually wrapping the emotion around you. Never become submerged in the emotion you portray. Remember, at all times, that it is the *rapport* you create between yourself and your audience that makes for the success of any evening; the listener must share in the experience or it has no value and consequently evinces no response. The audience has as much a part in creating a mood as the performer. The performer who does all the work fails in an important phase.

The elocutionary objective of this poem is to be two people. You must portray the lady and her prey in contrasting characterization. In the first two stanzas, the "helpless" one is the girl; in the last paragraph the situation is reversed.

Note that this poem is surrounded by quotation marks. This means a complete use of characterization of the participants. The "says I," "says Mary" lines must be absorbed into the characterization of the person who is reading; otherwise you will achieve only a jerky and off-balance quality. In the last stanzas, give just a touch of desperation to the young man. When he winds up his four-line appearance, wipe away the tears from Mary and with sweet helpfulness lead the young man to his seemingly impossible, but actually inevitable fate. Mary's last lines must have assurance and be filled with the poise she had been concealing. Have fun with this piece.

A SIMPLE PRAYER

St. Francis of Assisi

Lord, make me an instrument of Thy Peace. Where there is hatred, let me sow love. Where there is injury, pardon. Where there is doubt, faith. Where there is despair, hope. Where there is darkness, light. Where there is sadness, joy.

O Divine Master, grant that I may not so much seek to be consoled as to console; to be understood as to understand; to be loved, as to love; for it is in giving that we receive, it is in pardoning that we are pardoned, and it is in dying that we are born to Eternal Life.

IN judicial matters, one receives the injunction to appear before the court with "clean hands." Here is a work by clean hands, and a clear conscience. It cannot possibly be used as the peace offering of a sinner, but is intended as a bulwark of a good person's continued peace of mind. Too often are prayers used as a temporary sedative to a soul in need of hospitalization. This simple prayer is a re-affirmation of a way of life and not a begging message. Take care not to overwork the verbs in this piece. There is a serenity and an assurance about this. It is relaxed, completely relaxed.

The poem's first stanza is written with each sentence in two parts; one acts as the answer to the other. Pause between contrasting words such as "despair—hope," "darkness—light." In the second stanza, place your emphasis on the word "to" each time it is used in the "answer" part of the sentence. Thus: "To be loved (pause) as *to* love.

As an exercise in interpretation, this work offers challenges that are both elocutionary and spiritual. This is one piece about which we offer the suggestion: "Live the part."

STANZAS FOR MUSIC

George Gordon, Lord Byron

There be none of Beauty's daughters
   With a magic like thee;
And like music on the waters
   Is thy sweet voice to me:
When, as if its sound were causing
The charmèd ocean's pausing,
The waves lie still and gleaming,
And the lulled winds seem dreaming.

And the midnight moon is weaving
   Her bright chain o'er the deep,
Whose breast is gently heaving,
   As an infant's asleep:
So the spirit bows before thee,
To listen and adore thee;
With a full but soft emotion,
Like the swell of Summer's ocean

Have you ever seen a couple, completely in love, on a dance floor? They barely move around; they are completely unconscious of the other dancers. And perhaps if his lips are moving he might logically, if there be logic at such moments, be breathing this poem into his beloved's ears. This poem cannot be recited, it must be breathed. It is a poem designed for the table of a tête à tête and not for the platform of the performer; it achieves validity when the audience is limited to one. Don't try to matriculate on this work until you have had a preliminary experience with a romance. Love is an elective course.

This is a work almost devoid of motion. The waves are made to lie still, the breast is gently heaving, the images are all quiet and soft. Yet the emotion is the antithesis of the motion. This is a poem of deep and sincere feeling. The alchemy that transforms it into the Spoken Word challenges you to express, but to control, this feeling.

Don't attempt it unless the time, the place, the moments are right—not to mention the girl.

SONG

John Suckling

I prithee send me back my heart,
  Since I cannot have thine:
For if from yours you will not part,
  Why then shouldst thou have mine?

Yet now I think on't, let it lie,
  To find it were in vain,
For thou hast a thief in either eye
  Would steal it back again.

Why should two hearts in one breast lie
  And yet not lodge together?
O love, where is thy sympathy,
  If thus our breasts thou sever?

But love is such a mystery,
  I cannot find it out:
For when I think I'm best resolved,
  I then am most in doubt.

Then farewell care, and farewell woe!
  I will no longer pine;
For I'll believe I have her heart,
  As much as she hath mine.

IT is rare that one finds the combination of bookkeeping and romance that is woven into the design of this poem. Suckling in alternate stanzas is angered at unrequited love and philosophic about his lend-lease arrangement. One suspects that the poet is more in love with love, than in love. This relationship is a production that has little chance for a lengthy run, and soon will be stored in a Cain's warehouse of failures.

In reading this poem aloud you must alternate between anger and resignation. The first and third stanzas are the work of a pleasing man who burns with the unfairness of an unreciprocal trade treaty. The second, fourth, and fifth groupings are a complete reversal; the poet becomes the resigned philosopher. The anger comes in those two stanzas because the author treats his love as a personal matter. In the other three, he treats love in its broader sense.

Perhaps if you will visualize the following setting you will find an easy road to interpretation. Picture the poet, with pen in hand, writing a letter to his lady. At the end of the first stanza, he puts his pen—or was it a quill, Mr. Suckling?—down and thinks about it. Then at the third stanza, he picks it up again and again directly addresses the lady. Down goes the pen for the fourth, and at the fifth stanza, he tears up the writing paper. The first and third stanzas are intense, almost angry. The others are read with a light and cynical manner.

WHEN I WAS ONE-AND-TWENTY

A. E. Housman

When I was one-and-twenty
I heard a wise man say,
"Give crowns and pounds and guineas
But not your heart away;
Give pearls away and rubies
But keep your fancy free."
But I was one-and-twenty,
No use to talk to me.

When I was one-and-twenty
I heard him say again,
"The heart out of the bosom
Was never given in vain;
'Tis paid with sighs a-plenty
And sold for endless rue."
And I am two-and-twenty,
And oh, 'tis true ,'tis true.

HAVE you ever been caught in the act of swiping a cookie out of its hiding place? Pretty much, that is the position of our hero in this poem. He is warned, he transgresses, he is caught. He has no alibi but must enter a plea of guilty and he does it with good humor. Here is a man who not only learned his lesson but had it, too.

The dramatic trick of this piece is in the years —twenty-one and twenty-two. The first fourteen lines are the bill of particulars; the last two, the confession. Despite the even division of the lines, treat this work as though the poem were divided in the two sections outlined in the previous sentence. The pace is brisk, but not too fast. The wise man's remarks need characterization; they are warnings and should be spoken with an older vocal quality than the rest. At the end of the sixth line come to a complete stop. And then, like the young boy at the cookie bowl, smile the last two lines in your most rueful manner. These two lines call for a slow pace. One doesn't plead guilty with assurance.

SHERIDAN'S RIDE

Thomas Buchanan Read

Up from the South at the break of day,
Bringing to Winchester fresh dismay,
The affrighted air with a shudder bore,
Like a herald in haste, to the chieftain's door,
The terrible grumble, and rumble, and roar,
Telling the battle was on once more,
And Sheridan twenty miles away.

And wider still those billows of war
Thundered along the horizon's bar;
And louder yet into Winchester rolled
The roar of that red sea uncontrolled,
Making the blood of the listener cold,
As he thought of the stake in that fiery fray,
And Sheridan twenty miles away.

But there is a road from Winchester town,
A good, broad highway leading down;
And there, through the flush of the morning light,
A steed as black as the steed of night

Was seen to pass, as with eagle flight;
As if he knew the terrible need,
He stretched away with the utmost speed;
Hills rose and fell; but his heart was gay,
With Sheridan fifteen miles away.

Still sprung from those swift hoofs, thundering South,
The dust, like smoke from the cannon's mouth;
Or the trail of a comet, sweeping faster and faster,
Foreboding to traitors the doom of disaster,
The heart of the steed and the heart of the master
Were beating like prisoners assaulting their walls,
Impatient to be where the battlefield calls;
Every nerve of the charger was strained to full play,
With Sheridan only ten miles away.

Under his spurning feet the road
Like an arrowy Alpine river flowed,
And the landscape sped away behind
Like an ocean flying before the wind,
And the steed, like a barque fed with furnace fire,
Swept on, with his wild eye full of ire.
But lo! he is nearing his heart's desire;
He is snuffing the smoke of the roaring fray,
With Sheridan only five miles away.

The first that the general saw were the groups
Of stragglers, and then the retreating troops;
What was done? What to do? A glance told him both,
Then striking his spurs, with a terrible oath,
He dashed down the line 'mid a storm of huzzas,
And the wave of retreat checked its course there,
    because
The sight of the master compelled it to pause.
With foam and with dust the black charger was gray;
By the flash of his eye and the red nostril's play,
He seemed to the whole great army to say,
"I have brought you Sheridan all the way
From Winchester down to save the day!"

Hurrah! Hurrah for Sheridan!
Hurrah! Hurrah for horse and man!
And when their statues are placed on high,
Under the dome of the Union sky,
The American soldier's Temple of Fame;
There with the glorious general's name,
Be it said, in letters both bold and bright,
"Here is the steed that saved the day,
By carrying Sheridan into the fight,
From Winchester, twenty miles away!"

THERE is a standard scene in movies involving cops and robbers. You recall the detective with fresh evidence hurtling through the countryside over Zanuck-made obstacles, racing against time to reach the governor and get a pardon for an innocent man who is about to be electrocuted. From time to time, he glances at his watch: Twenty minutes to twelve— fifteen minutes to twelve—ten minutes to twelve—the suspense is terrific! That same dramatic situation is found in Sheridan's Ride. First he is twenty miles away, then fifteen, then ten, then five! Will he make it?

This is as much an exclamation point as a poem. It derives its best effect from tremendous speed. It moves at break-neck pace. The dramatic device is the variant that makes the speed possible. For the horse and its rider rush down the road to be brought to complete stops while one checks the mileage. Each time the distance is given (you'll find it listed in the last line of each of the first five stanzas) pull up to a complete and abrupt stop after "Sheridan" and give the distance slowly and dramatically. Immediately spur yourself on into the mad dash for the battle—to pull up sharply as you reach the last line of the next stanza.

The very last stanza calls for a drastically slower pace than the rest of the poem. It is practically the inscription on the immobile statue it predicts.

RECESSIONAL

Rudyard Kipling

God of our fathers, known of old,
  Lord of our far-flung battle-line,
Beneath whose awful hand we hold
  Dominion over palm and pine—
Lord God of Hosts, be with us yet,
Lest we forget — lest we forget!

The tumult and the shouting dies;
  The captains and the kings depart:
Still stands Thine ancient sacrifice,
  An humble and a contrite heart.
Lord God of Hosts, be with us yet,
Lest we forget — lest we forget!

Far-called, our navies melt away;
  On dune and headland sinks the fire:
Lo, all our pomp of yesterday
  Is one with Nineveh and Tyre!
Judge of the Nations, spare us yet,
Lest we forget — lest we forget!

If, drunk with sight of power, we loose
  Wild tongues that have not Thee in awe,
Such boastings as the Gentiles use,
  Or lesser breeds without the Law—
Lord God of Hosts, be with us yet,
Lest we forget — lest we forget!

For heathen heart that puts her trust
  In reeking tube and iron shard,
All valiant dust that builds on dust,
  And, guarding, calls not Thee to guard,
For frantic boast and foolish word—
Thy Mercy on Thy People, Lord!

W̶RITTEN during the "noblest" years of Britain's expansion, this poem is not so much a prayer as a warning. This is a poem of rebuke, a warning of decay. Kipling rubs the conscience of the English people and suggests that perhaps the sun (power) *will* set on the English empire. In a world that searches and fumbles for peace, this lesson calling on people to heed the spiritual values of living is applicable to the Victorian age as a prophesy and to our times as a political brake. Here is a poem that could be read at the start of each meeting of the United Nations. Kipling suggests, in advance, that perhaps there is a fifth Power possessing a veto.

There is an interesting device which Kipling uses that must be understood by the reader before proceeding. In categorizing the world's lust for power and possession as a rejection of God, Kipling appeals to the Diety for help and pardon. It is around the lack and need of God that this work achieves its dramatic impact. While cataloguing the acts of power, Kipling ties on to each stanza a petition for help. The reading of the petition is the challenge of the poem. Don't make the mistake of over-emotionalizing the plea "Lord God of Hosts, be with us yet." It is delivered more with the humility of a head bowed with shame than a sinner grovelling on his knees, waving his arms wildly. The excessive beggary of a whining reading is too obviously a surface plea for mercy rather than a willingness to reform. It is sacrilegeous to make your prayer a bombardment, the keynote is humility.

The listing of the empire's triumphs (the map is covered from the pines of the North to the palms of the South) should be read with the roundness and grandeur one associates with the Victorian era. When, in each paragraph, the prayer motif is introduced, break off the rolling tones and switch to the simple and humble tone previously suggested. It is as though you suddenly walked out of a twenty-one gun salute into the quiet chapel of a country church.

WHEN I WAS A LAD

W. S. Gilbert

When I was a lad I served a term
As office boy to an attorney's firm.
I cleaned the windows and I swept the floor,
And I polished up the handle of the big front door.
  I polished up that handle so carefullee
  That now I am the Ruler of the Queen's Navee!

As office boy I made such a mark
That they gave me the post of a junior clerk.
I served the writs with a smile so bland,
And I copied all the letters in a big round hand —
  I copied all the letters in a hand so free,
  That now I am the Ruler of the Queen's Navee!

In serving writs I made such a name
Than an articled clerk I soon became;
I wore clean collars and a brand-new suit
For the pass-examination at the Institute.
  And that pass-examination did so well for me,
  That now I am the Ruler of the Queen's Navee!

Of legal knowledge I acquired such a grip
That they took me into the partnership
And that junior partnership, I ween,
Was the only ship I ever had seen.
　　But that kind of ship so suited me,
　　That now I am the Ruler of the Queen's Navee!

I grew so rich that I was sent
By a pocket borough into Parliament.
I always voted at my party's call,
And I never thought of thinking for myself at all.
　　I thought so little, they rewarded me
　　By making me the Ruler of the Queen's Navee!

Now, landsmen, all, whoever you may be,
If you want to rise to the top of the tree,
If your soul isn't fettered to an office stool,
Be careful to be guided by this golden rule—
　　Stick close to your desk and never go to sea,
　　And you *all* may be Rulers of the Queen's Navee!

(*from* PINAFORE)

As the Ham and Eggs of the Savoy Opera, Gilbert and Sullivan have achieved a partnership that has resulted in their being classed as Siamese Twins. In laying aside Mr. Sullivan's music, this annotator suggests that Ham is still a desirable item even when not served with Eggs. As sparkling nuggets of satire, Gilbert's lyrics are among the brilliant poems of our language. In treating them as poems rather than as lyrics there is a tendency to recall the tempo and music of Sullivan's music, with the reader practically looking for a conductor to start him off with a downbeat. But once this mental hazard is passed, the fun of Gilbert is a delightful exercise.

Starting with a pace that must necessarily be slower than the tempo markings of the musical performance, an interesting effect is created by taking a complete break after the first four lines of each stanza and then reading the last two very, very slowly. Try it.

Since the leading player is a real caricature, your voice must be caricatured. Don't spoil this piece by overdoing the caricaturization. The "Ruler of the Queen's Navee" is a rather likeable, simple soul who is the tool of Gilbert's satire; remember, please, that he is the nail and not the hammer. Give your voice some of that Arthur Treacher quality and play the piece with his dead pan. In the second verse, "clerk" is pronounced "clark."

If you enjoy this treatment of G and S lyrics, thumb through your Savoyard repertory and take other famous patter songs. Slow them down and see how much fun it is "Stompin' at the Savoy."

IF IT HAD NOT BEEN FOR THESE THINGS
Bartolomeo Vanzetti

If it had not been for these things,
I might have live out my life
Talking on street corners
    To scorning men.

I might have die
    Unmarked
    Unknown
    A failure.

Now we are not a failure.

This is our career
And
Our triumph!

Never
In our full life
Can we hope to do such work
    For tolerance
    For justice
    For man's understanding of ma
As now we do
By an accident.

Our words—
Our lives—
Our pains—
      Nothing!

The taking of our lives
Lives
      of a good shoemaker
      and a poor fish peddler
All!

That last moment belongs to us.
That agony is our triumph.

LANGUAGE in itself is a parasite that feeds on thoughts of men. By themselves, words are useless tools that can carve only when they are matched with the material of honest ideas. Vanzetti (now conceded to be innocent of the charges which sent him to the death cell) was an uneducated man, unskilled in grammar. But after being convicted, he made a reply to Judge Thayer which has become famous. He pushed out an eloquent speech, full of honest poetry. Here the spoken English is broken English. The right words are subordinate to the right thoughts. Because this speech by the untutored shoemaker is as dramatic as anything that has ever been written and thus earns a place in the English curriculums of many schools, it rates a place in this volume of nimble word-users. It is here, where language is stripped to its essentials of emotion, that we readily appreciate the architecture of honest sentiment and may logically challenge a writer's work by the sampling of this sincerity.

Vanzetti has a hard time putting these words together. His thought is clear in his mind but the words are painfully shaped to the mould of his emotions. When you read this piece, *be* Vanzetti. Reach out for the words; find them after a search. The piece, which we have arranged in a semblance of blank verse, opens quietly and simply. When you reach the third stanza, "Now we are not a failure," light the fire and let the flames burst forth. Carry this strong emotion straight through until the final two lines. Return, then, to the simplicity and quietness of the opening two stanzas.

THE BALLAD OF READING GAOL
Oscar Wilde

I

He did not wear his scarlet coat,
  For blood and wine are red,
And blood and wine were on his hands
  When they found him with the dead,
The poor dead woman whom he loved,
  And murdered in her bed.

He walked amongst the Trial Men
  In a suit of shabby gray;
A cricket cap was on his head,
  And his step seemed light and gay;
But I never saw a man who looked
  So wistfully at the day.

I never saw a man who looked
  With such a wistful eye
Upon that little tent of blue
  Which prisoners call the sky,
And at every drifting cloud that went
  With sails of silver by.

I walked, with other souls in pain,
    Within another ring,
And was wondering if the man had done
    A great or little thing,
When a voice behind me whispered low,
    "That fellow's got to swing."

Dear Christ! the very prison walls
    Suddenly seemed to reel,
And the sky above my head became
    Like a casque of scorching steel;
And, though I was a soul in pain,
    My pain I could not feel.

I only knew what hunted thought
    Quickened his step, and why
He looked upon the garish day
    With such a wistful eye;
The man had killed the thing he loved,
    And so he had to die.

Yet each man kills the thing he loves,
    By each let this be heard,
Some do it with a bitter look,
    Some with a flattering word,
The coward does it with a kiss,
    The brave man with a sword!

Some kill their love when they are young,
  And some when they are old;
Some strangle with the hands of Lust,
  Some with the hands of Gold:
The kindest use a knife, because
  The dead so soon grow cold.

Some love too little, some too long,
  Some sell, and others buy;
Some do the deed with many tears,
  And some without a sigh:
For each man kills the thing he loves,
  Yet each man does not die.

He does not die a death of shame
  On a day of dark disgrace,
Nor have a noose about his neck,
  Nor a cloth upon his face,
Nor drop feet foremost through the floor
  Into an empty space.

He does not sit with silent men
  Who watch him night and day;
Who watch him when he tries to weep,
  And when he tries to pray;
Who watch him lest himself should rob
  The prison of its prey.

He does not wake at dawn to see
Dread figures throng his room,
The shivering Chaplain robed in white,
The Sheriff stern with gloom,
And the Governor all in shiny black,
With the yellow face of Doom.

He does not rise in piteous haste
To put on convict-clothes,
While some coarse-mouthed Doctor gloats, and notes
Each new and nerve-twitched pose,
Fingering a watch whose little ticks
Are like horrible hammer-blows.

He does not know that sickening thirst
That sands one's throat, before
The hangman with his gardener's gloves
Slips through the padded door,
And binds one with three leathern thongs
That the throat may thirst no more.

He does not bend his head to hear
The Burial Office read,
Nor, while the terror of his soul
Tells him he is not dead,
Cross his own coffin, as he moves
Into the hideous shed.

He does not stare upon the air
  Through a little roof of glass:
He does not pray with lips of clay
  For his agony to pass;
Nor feel upon his shuddering cheek
  The kiss of Caiaphas.

II

Six weeks our guardsman walked the yard
  In the suit of shabby gray:
His cricket cap was on his head,
  And his step seemed light and gay,
But I never saw a man who looked
  So wistfully at the day.

I never saw a man who looked
  With such a wistful eye
Upon that little tent of blue
  Which prisoners call the sky.
And at every wandering cloud that trailed
  Its ravelled fleeces by.

He did not wring his hands, as do
　Those witless men who dare
To try to rear the changeling Hope
　In the cave of black Despair:
He only looked upon the sun,
　And drank the morning air.

He did not wring his hands nor weep,
　Nor did he peek or pine,
But he drank the air as though it held
　Some heathful anodyne;
With open mouth he drank the sun
　As though it had been wine!

And I and all the souls in pain
　Who tramped the other ring,
Forgot if we ourselves had done
　A great or little thing,
And watched with gaze of dull amaze
　The man who had to swing.

And strange it was to see him pass
　With a step so light and gay,
And strange it was to see him look
　So wistfully at the day,
And strange it was to think that he
　Had such a debt to pay.

For oak and elm have pleasant leaves
   That in the spring-time shoot:
But grim to see is the gallows-tree,
   With its adder-bitten root,
And, green or dry, a man must die
   Before it bears its fruit.

The loftiest place is that seat of grace
   For which all worldlings try:
But who would stand in hempen band
   Upon a scaffold high,
And through a murderer's collar take
   His last look at the sky?

It is sweet to dance to violins
   When Love and Life are fair:
To dance to flutes, to dance to lutes
   Is delicate and rare:
But it is not sweet with nimble feet
   To dance upon the air!

So with curious eyes and sick surmise
   We watched him day by day,
And wondered if each one of us
   Would end the self-same way,
For none can tell to what red Hell
   His sightless soul may stray.

At last the dead man walked no more
  Amongst the Trial Men,
And I knew that he was standing up
  In the black dock's dreadful pen,
And that never would I see his face
  In God's sweet world again.

Like two doomed ships that pass in storm
  We had crossed each other's way:
But we made no sign, we said no word,
  We had no word to say;
For we did not meet in the holy night,
  But in the shameful day.

A prison wall was round us both,
  Two outcast men we were:
The world had thrust us from its heart,
  And God from out His care:
And the iron gin that waits for Sin
  Had caught us in its snare.

III

In Debtors' Yard the stones are hard,
    And the dripping wall is high,
So it was there he took the air
    Beneath the leaden sky.
And by each side a Warder walked,
    For fear the man might die.

Or else he sat with those who watched
    His anguish night and day;
Who watched him when he rose to weep,
    And when he crouched to pray;
Who watched him lest himself should rob
    Their scaffold of its prey.

The Governor was strong upon
    The Regulations Act:
The Doctor said that Death was but
    A scientific fact:
And twice a day the Chaplain called,
    And left a little tract.

And twice a day he smoked his pipe,
    And drank his quart of beer:
His soul was resolute, and held
    No hiding-place for fear;
He often said that he was glad
    The hangman's hands were near.

But why he said so strange a thing
    No Warder dared to ask:
For he to whom a watcher's doom
    Is given as his task,
Must set a lock upon his lips,
    And make his face a mask.

Or else he might be moved, and try
    To comfort or console:
And what should Human Pity do
    Pent up in Murderers' Hole?
What word of grace in such a place
    Could help a brother's soul?

With slouch and swing around the ring
    We trod the Fools' Parade!
We did not care: we knew we were
    The Devil's Own Brigade:
And shaven head and feet of lead
    Make a merry masquerade.

We tore the tarry rope to shreds
    With blunt and bleeding nails;
We rubbed the doors, and scrubbed the floors,
    And cleaned the shining rails:
And, rank by rank, we soaped the plank,
    And clattered with the pails.

We sewed the sacks, we broke the stones.
  We turned the dusty drill:
We banged the tins, and bawled the hymns,
  And sweated on the mill:
But in the heart of every man
  Terror was lying still.

So still it lay that every day
  Crawled like a weed-clogged wave:
And we forgot the bitter lot
  That waits for fool and knave,
Till once, as we tramped in from work,
  We passed an open grave.

With yawning mouth the yellow hole
  Gaped for a living thing;
The very mud cried out for blood
  To the thirsty asphalt ring:
And we knew that ere one dawn grew fair
  Some prisoner had to swing.

Right in we went, with soul intent
  On Death and Dread and Doom:
The hangman, with his little bag,
  Went shuffling through the gloom:
And each man trembled as he crept
  Into his numbered tomb.

That night the empty corridors
  Were full of forms of Fear,
And up and down the iron town
  Stole feet we could not hear,
And through the bars that hide the stars
  White faces seemed to peer.

He lay as one who lies and dreams
  In a pleasant meadow-land,
The watchers watched him as he slept,
  And could not understand
How one could sleep so sweet a sleep
  With a hangman close at hand.

But there is no sleep when men must weep
  Who never yet have wept:
So we—the fool, the fraud, the knave—
  That endless vigil kept,
And through each brain on hands of pain
  Another's terror crept.

Alas! it is a fearful thing
  To feel another's guilt!
For, right within, the sword of Sin
  Pierced to its poisoned hilt,
And as molten lead were the tears we shed
  For the blood we had not spilt.

The Warders with their shoes of felt
  Crept by each padlocked door,
And peeped and saw, with eyes of awe,
  Gray figures on the floor,
And wonder why men knelt to pray
  Who never prayed before.

All through the night we knelt and prayed,
  Mad mourners of a corse!
The troubled plumes of midnight were
  The plumes upon the hearse:
And bitter wine upon a sponge
  Was the savor of Remorse.

The gray cock crew, the red cock crew,
  But never came the day:
And crooked shapes of Terror crouched,
  In the corners where we lay:
And each evil sprite that walks by night
  Before us seemed to play.

They glided past, they glided fast,
  Like travelers through a mist:
They mocked the moon in a rigadoon
  Of delicate turn and twist,
And with formal pace and loathsome grace
  The phantoms kept their tryst.

With mop and mow, we saw them go,
   Slim shadows hand in hand:
About, about, in ghostly rout
   They trod a saraband:
And the damned grotesques made arabesques,
   Like the wind upon the sand!

With the pirouettes of marionettes,
   They tripped on pointed tread:
But with flutes of Fear they filled the ear,
   As their grisly masque they led,
And loud they sang, and long they sang,
   For they sang to wake the dead.

"Oho!" they cried, "The World is wide,
   But fettered limbs go lame!
And once, or twice, to throw the dice
   Is a gentlemanly game;
But he does not win who plays with Sin
   In the secret House of Shame."

No things of air these antics were,
   That frolicked with such glee:
To men whose lives were held in gyves,
   And whose feet might not go free,
Ah! wounds of Christ! they were livings things,
   Most terrible to see.

Around, around, they waltzed and wound;
    Some wheeled in smirking pairs;
With the mincing step of a demirep
    Some sidled up the stairs:
And with subtle sneer, and fawning leer,
    Each helped us at our prayers.

The morning wind began to moan,
    But still the night went on:
Through its giant loom the web of gloom
    Crept till each thread was spun:
And, as we prayed, we grew afraid
    Of the Justice of the Sun.

The moaning wind went wandering round
    The weeping prison-wall:
Till like a wheel of turning steel
    We felt the minutes crawl:
O moaning wind! what had we done
    To have such a seneschal?

At last I saw the shadowed bars,
    Like a lattice wrought in lead,
Move right across the whitewashed wall
    That faced my three-plank bed,
And I knew that somewhere in the world
    God's dreadful dawn was red.

At six o'clock we cleaned our cells,
  At seven all was still,
But the sough and swing of a mighty wing
  The prison seemed to fill,
For the Lord of Death with icy breath
  Had entered in to kill.

He did not pass in purple pomp,
  Nor ride a moon-white steed.
Three yards of cord and a sliding board
  Are all the gallows' need:
So with rope of shame the Herald came
  To do the secret deed.

We were as men who through a fen
  Of filthy darkness grope:
We did not dare to breathe a prayer,
  Or to give our anguish scope:
Something was dead in each of us,
  And what was dead was Hope.

For Man's grim Justice goes its way,
  And will not swerve aside:
It slays the weak, it slays the strong,
  It has a deadly stride:
With iron heel it slays the strong,
  The monstrous parricide!

We waited for the stroke of eight:
  Each tongue was thick with thirst:
For the stroke of eight is the stroke of Fate
  That makes a man accursed,
And Fate will use a running noose
  For the best man and the worst.

We had no other thing to do,
  Save to wait for the sign to come:
So, like things of stone in a valley lone,
  Quiet we sat and dumb:
But each man's heart beat thick and quick,
  Like a madman on a drum!

With sudden shock the prison clock
  Smote on the shivering air,
And from all the gaol rose up a wail
  Of impotent despair,
Like the sound that frightened marshes hear
  From some leper in his lair.

And as one sees most fearful things
  In the crystal of a dream,
We saw the greasy hempen rope
  Hooked to the blackened beam,
And heard the prayer the hangman's snare
  Strangled into a scream.

And all the woe that moved him so
  That he gave that bitter cry,
And the wild regrets, and the bloody sweats,
  None knew so well as I:
For he who lives more lives than one
  More deaths than one must die.

IV

There is no chapel on the day
  On which they hang a man:
The Chaplain's heart is far too sick,
  Or his face is far too wan,
Or there is that written in his eyes
  Which none should look upon.

So they kept us close till nigh on noon,
  And then they rang the bell,
And the Warders with their jingling keys
  Opened each listening cell,
And down the iron stair we tramped,
  Each from his separate Hell.

Out into God's sweet air we went,
    But not in wonted way,
For this man's face was white with fear,
    And that man's face was gray,
And I never saw sad men who looked
    So wistfully at the day.

I never saw sad men who looked
    With such a wistful eye
Upon that little tent of blue
    We prisoners called the sky,
And at every careless cloud that passed
    In happy freedom by.

But there were those amongst us all
    Who walked with downcast head,
And knew that, had each got his due,
    They should have died instead:
He had but killed a thing that lived,
    Whilst they had killed the dead.

For he who sins a second time
    Wakes a dead soul to pain,
And draws it from its spotted shroud,
    And makes it bleed again,
And makes it bleed great gouts of blood,
    And makes it bleed in vain!

Like ape or clown, in monstrous garb
   With crooked arrows starred,
Silently we went round and round
   The slippery asphalt yard;
Silently we went round and round,
   And no man spoke a word.

Silently we went round and round,
   And through each hollow mind
The Memory of dreadful things
   Rushed like a dreadful wind,
And Horror stalked before each man,
   And Terror crept behind.

The Warders strutted up and down,
   And kept their herd of brutes,
Their uniforms were spick and span,
   And they wore their Sunday suits,
But we knew the work they had been at,
   By the quicklime on their boots.

For where a grave had opened wide,
   There was no grave at all:
Only a stretch of mud and sand
   By the hideous prison-wall,
And a little heap of burning lime,
   That the man should have his pall.

For he has a pall, this wretched man,
    Such as few men can claim:
Deep down below a prison-yard,
    Naked for greater shame,
He lies, with fetters on each foot,
    Wrapt in a sheet of flame!

And all the while the burning lime
    Eats flesh and bone away;
It eats the brittle bone by night,
    And the soft flesh by day,
It eats the flesh and bone by turns,
    But it eats the heart away.

For three long years they will not sow
    Or root or seedling there:
For three long years the unblessed spot
    Will sterile be and bare,
And look upon the wondering sky
    With unreproachful stare.

They think a murderer's heart would taint
    Each simple seed they sow.
It is not true! God's kindly earth
    Is kindlier than men know,
And the red rose would but blow more red,
    The white rose whiter blow.

Out of his mouth a red, red rose!
  Out of his heart a white!
For who can say by what strange way,
  Christ brings His will to light,
Since the barren staff the pilgrim bore
  Bloomed in the great Pope's sight?

But neither milk-white rose nor red
  May bloom in prison air;
The shard, the pebble, and the flint,
  Are what they give us there:
For flowers have been known to heal
  A common man's despair.

So never will wine-red rose or white,
  Petal by petal, fall
On that stretch of mud and sand that lies
  By the hideous prison-wall,
To tell the men who tramp the yard
  That God's Son died for all.

Yet though the hideous prison-wall
  Still hems him round and round,
And a spirit may not walk by night
  That is with fetters bound,
And a spirit may but weep that lies
  In such unholy ground.

He is at peace—this wretched man—
    At peace, or will be soon:
There is no thing to make him mad,
    Nor does Terror walk at noon,
For the lampless Earth in which he lies
    Has neither Sun nor Moon.

They hanged him as a beast is hanged:
    They did not even toll
A requiem that might have brought
    Rest to his startled soul,
But hurriedly they took him out,
    And hid him in a hole.

They stripped him of his canvas clothes,
    And gave him to the flies;
They mocked the swollen purple throat,
    And the stark and staring eyes;
And with laughter loud they heaped the shroud
    In which their convict lies.

The Chaplain would not kneel to pray
    By his dishonored grave:
Nor mark it with that blessed Cross
    That Christ for sinners gave,
Because the man was one of those
    Whom Christ came down to save.

Yet all is well; he has but passed,
   To Life's appointed bourne:
And alien tears will fill for him
   Pity's long-broken urn,
For his mourners will be outcast men,
   And outcasts always mourn.

V

I know not whether Laws be right,
   Or whether Laws be wrong;
All that we know who lie in gaol
   Is that the wall is strong;
And that each day is like a year,
   A year whose days are long.

But this I know, that every Law
   That men have made for Man,
Since first Man took his brother's life,
   And the sad world began,
But straws the wheat and saves the chaff
   With a most evil fan.

This too I know—and wise it were
  If each could know the same—
That every prison that men build
  Is built with bricks of shame,
And bound with bars lest Christ should see
  How men their brothers maim.

With bars they blur the gracious moon,
  And blind the goodly sun:
And they do well to hide their Hell,
  For in it things are done
That Son of God nor Son of Man
  Ever should look upon!

The vilest deeds like poison weeds
  Bloom well in prison-air:
It is only what is good in Man
  That wastes and withers there:
Pale Anguish keeps the heavy gate,
  And the Warder is Despair.

For they starve the little frightened child
  Till it weeps both night and day:
And they scourge the weak, and flog the fool,
  And gibe the old and gray,
And some grow mad, and all grow bad,
  And none a word may say.

Each narrow cell in which we dwell
    Is a foul and dark latrine.
And the fetid breath of living Death
    Chokes up each grated screen,
And all, but Lust, is turned to dust
    In Humanity's machine.

The brackish water that we drink
    Creeps with a loathsome slime,
And the bitter bread they weigh in scales
    Is full of chalk and lime,
And Sleep will not lie down, but walks
    Wild-eyed, and cries to Time.

But though lean Hunger and green Thirst
    Like asp with adder fight,
We have little care of prison fare,
    For what chills and kills outright
Is that every stone one lifts by day
    Becomes one's heart by night.

With midnight always in one's heart,
    And twilight in one's cell,
We turn the crank, or tear the rope,
    Each in his separate Hell,
And the silence is more awful far
    Than the sound of a brazen bell.

And never a human voice comes near
  To speak a gentle word:
And the eye that watches through the door
  Is pitiless and hard:
And by all forgot, we rot and rot,
  With soul and body marred.

And thus we rust Life's iron chain
  Degraded and alone:
And some men curse, and some men weep,
  And some men make no moan:
But God's eternal Laws are kind
  And break the heart of stone.

And every human heart that breaks,
  In prison-cell or yard,
Is as that broken box that gave
  Its treasure to the Lord,
And filled the unclean leper's house
  With the scent of costliest nard.

Ah! happy they whose hearts can break
  And peace of pardon win!
How else may man make straight his plan
  And cleanse his soul from Sin?
How else but through a broken heart
  May Lord Christ enter in?

And he of the swollen purple throat,
    And the stark and staring eyes
Waits for the holy hands that took
    The Thief to Paradise;
And a broken and a contrite heart
    The Lord will not despise.

The man in red who reads the Law
    Gave him three weeks of life,
Three little weeks in which to heal
    His soul of his soul's strife,
And cleanse from every blot of blood
    The hand that held the knife.

And with tears of blood he cleansed the hand,
    The hand that held the steel:
For only blood can wipe out blood,
    And only tears can heal:
And the crimson stain that was of Cain
    Became Christ's snow-white seal.

VI

In Reading gaol by Reading town
  There is a pit of shame,
And in it lies a wretched man
  Eaten by teeth of flame,
In a burning winding-sheet he lies,
  And his grave has got no name.

And there, till Christ call forth the dead,
  In silence let him lie:
No need to waste the foolish tear,
  Or heave the windy sigh:
The man had killed the thing he loved,
  And so he had to die.

And all men kill the thing they love,
  By all let this be heard,
Some do it with a bitter look,
  Some with a flattering word,
The coward does it with a kiss,
  The brave man with a sword!

O SCAR WILDE has defined the cynic as "the man who knows the price of everything, the value of nothing." Having cast the first stone, Mr. Wilde must hang by his own noose. He has the bitterness of all cynics; never hesitating to coin a phrase even if it meant damning a friend.

As an epigrammatist, Wilde was fluent and facetious, a professional wit who sometimes said what he meant, but on very few occasions meant what he said. His witty sayings were in all probability carefully rehearsed ad-libs, holding a sharply turned phrase in escrow until the propitious moment. His plays were amusing bits of fluff whose every character was his Charlie McCarthy. It was when the puppet strings were cut and Wilde found himself in the shabby gray of a prisoner's uniform that he wrote what critics consider his most sincere, and possibly his only sincere work. This is "The Ballad of Reading Gaol."

Wilde was sent to prison for statutory offenses of th criminal code resulting from a morals charge. While in prison he wrote this work which is a bitter presentation of a prisoner' mind. Wilde never considered himself a criminal, but rathe the inmate of a house of detention. This ballad, therefore, not so much a confession as an indictment against all of ma kind. Wilde is angered by being singled out for punishmer Here is the bitterness of a man who has convinced himself th the world is evil; that all men are evil. He rails against t laws because they choose to punish a few men when a wh world of guilty men remains free of the restrictions of ba And so his pardon, if he is to get one, will not come by a reformation or atonement, but by an indictment of the wo He asks for his passport back into the "free" world because would only be joining other sinners. The legal principle that a man is innocent until proven guilty has no place in Wilde's philosophy; all men are guilty; conviction is not a confirmation of guilt but the action of being caught.

This ballad is printed not to sway you with its philosophy. If enough men of good faith had read "Mein Kampf" the menace of Hitler would have been more readily apparent. As a stimulation of discussion, this ballad has great possibilities. Too often has it been presented as a heroic piece of suffering, while actually, as a superb literary craftsman, Wilde has only coated his cynical philosophy with a smooth lacquer. He is without belief and so his invocation of the Deity is a shocking piece of hypocrisy. A man who labels all things as evil cannot expect redemption despite his avowal of waiting till Christ will raise the dead. Starting off with the premise that this is a ballad of bitterness, and rejecting the idea of labelling it a claim for justice, the reader will have an overall quality set for the reading of this work. It is a challenge not only confined to the philosophical field, but to the elocutionary. As a long work, it has to be carefully handled to keep the embers of your listeners' interest from dying out. The reader will not have much opportunity for change of pace. The variations will come in terms of changes of intensity. There is very little action in the poem. One develops a sense of motion not from change of tempo but a change of time.

In this very subjective poem there are no long shots—refer to the motion picture and television techniques—but series of closeups. Intensity is the key to the reading—the intensity of bitterness.

In labelling this piece a ballad, Wilde is indicating the use of repeated choruses to achieve dramatic effects. The stanza beginning "Each man kills the thing he loves" is used again and again like the refrain of an ancient ballad. The repetition is an excellent dramatic device. It is most effective to recite these refrains in the same manner each time they appear.

The work is written in a minor key. But the sadness is not a clue to you for a decision on tempo; bitterness is an active form of hate. It has an energy that calls for a fairly brisk pace. There are moments, particularly when Wilde bares his fear of death by his reactions to the hanging of the murderer, when you can slow down.

In a sense this is a terrifying piece. It is a cunning and twisted mind that wrote it. Just as Wilde twisted a phrase into a bon mot, so he twists the concept of good and evil for his own purposes. Beware of his literary camouflage and score a direct hit on the objective of an effective reading by bringing into your interpretation the hate and bitterness of a doomed man. This is the autobiography of a diseased mind.

THE TIME I'VE LOST IN WOOING

Thomas Moore

The time I've lost in wooing,
In watching and pursuing
   The light that lies
   In woman's eyes,
Has been my heart's undoing.
Though Wisdom oft has sought me,
I scorned the lore she brought me,
   My only books
   Were women's looks,
And folly's all they taught me.

Her smile when Beauty granted,
I hung with gaze enchanted,
   Like him the sprite
   Whom maids by night
Oft meet in glen that's haunted.
Like him, too, Beauty won me;

But when the spell was on me,
    If once their ray
    Was turned away,
O! winds could not outrun me.

And are those follies going?
And is my proud heart growing
    Too cold or wise
    For brilliant eyes
Again to set it glowing?
No—vain, alas! th' endeavor
From bonds so sweet to sever;—
    Poor Wisdom's chance
    Against a glance
Is now as weak as ever.

THIS Don Juan has matriculated in the school of Flirtation and won his varsity letter. If this were a bitter man, the poem would be an epitaph rather than the battle cry that it is. He is a happy cynic who glories in his weakness despite his analytical ability to rally reason to his cause. He uses his logic to admit the pleasantness of his weakness. I rather like the man who is portrayed here. He sounds like good company.

The helpful fact in reading this one is the illogical use of Logic. The man starts off with the assumption that his weakness for women is wrong. But like Oscar Wilde he is quite willing to agree to get rid of temptation by yielding to it. This is not good long range philosophy, but for the young it presents a possible directive for enjoyment. This man, like so many of us, is convinced that he really is in command of the situation. He has resolved the fact that his weakness for women is predicated on the simple fact that he enjoys it. He has overlooked the real point of the matter . . . he may think he's the fisherman, but actually he's the fish.

This is more a toast than a poem. Here is a literate, gallant, graceful, charming man. The adjectives are the directives for reading aloud. Guide yourself by the punctuation marks; they are, in this case, an excellent road map to proper interpretation.

I WILL LIFT UP MINE EYES
UNTO THE HILLS

(From The Book of Psalms)

I will lift up mine eyes unto the hills, from whence cometh my help.

My help cometh from the Lord, which made heaven and earth.

He will not suffer thy foot to be moved: he that keepeth thee will not slumber.

Behold, he that keepeth Israel shall neither slumber nor sleep.

The Lord is thy keeper: the Lord is thy shade upon thy right hand.

The sun shall not smite thee by day, nor the moon by night.

The Lord shall preserve thee from all evil: he shall preserve thy soul.

The Lord shall preserve thy going out and th coming in from this time forth, and even for evermor

IVIDE this psalm into two parts. The first eight lines are an affirmation of belief; the second eight are lines of advice. In the first the verbs call for emphasis. In the second the tone is softer, the remarks more direct.

Underline "lift up" in the first line; "cometh" and "made" in the third; "not" in both the third and fourth lines. "Behold" should be read strongly with a pause after you sound it. Give equal emphasis to "slumber" and "sleep" in the fourth paragraph.

In the last eight lines give special attention to the word "thy." Here the emphasis should be warm; you are speaking to a friend. Be careful not to read this psalm in a jerky manner that will result from lining up each paragraph as a separate thought. Each is part of the whole. Take a long pause after the fourth paragraph and then direct your reading into the soft and warm channel suggested.

Simplicity and gentleness are the two keywords to this work.

HOW THEY BROUGHT THE GOOD NEWS FROM GHENT TO AIX

Robert Browning

I sprang to the stirrup, and Joris, and he;
I galloped, Dirck galloped, we galloped all three;
"Good speed!" cried the watch, as the gate-bolts
  undrew;
"Speed!" echoed the wall to us galloping through;
Behind shut the postern, the lights sank to rest,
And into the midnight we galloped abreast.

Not a word to each other; we kept the great pace
Neck by neck, stride by stride, never changing our place;
I turned in my saddle and made its girths tight,
Then shortened each stirrup, and set the pique right,
Rebuckled the check-strap, chained slacker the bit,
Nor galloped less steadily Roland a whit.

'Twas moonset at starting; but while we drew near
Lokeren, the cocks crew and twilight dawned clear;
At Boom, a great yellow star came out to see;
At Düffeld, 'twas morning as plain as could be;
And from Mecheln church-steeple we heard the half
  chime,
So Joris broke silence with, "Yet there is time!"

At Aershot, up leaped of a sudden the sun,
And against him the cattle stood black every one,
To stare through the mist at us galloping past,
And I saw my stout galloper Roland at last,
With resolute shoulders, each butting away
The haze, as some bluff river headland its spray:

And his low head and crest, just one sharp ear bent
   back
For my voice, and the other pricked out on his track;
And one eye's black intelligence,—ever that glance
O'er its white edge at me, his own master, askance!
And the thick heavy spume-flakes which aye and anon
His fierce lips shook upwards in galloping on.

By Hasselt, Dirck groaned; and cried Joris "Stay spur!
Your Roos galloped bravely, the fault's not in her,
We'll remember at Aix"—for one heard the quick
   wheeze
Of her chest, saw the stretched neck and staggering
   knees,
And sunk tail, and horrible heave of the flank,
As down on her haunches she shuddered and sank.

So, we were left galloping, Joris and I,
Past Looz and past Tongres, no cloud in the sky;
The broad sun above laughed a pitiless laugh,

'Neath our feet broke the brittle bright stubble like
    chaff;
Till over by Dalhem a dome-spire sprang white,
And "Gallop," gasped Joris, "for Aix is in sight!

"How they'll greet us!"—and all in a moment his roan
Rolled neck and croup over, lay dead as a stone;
And there was my Roland to bear the whole weight
Of the news which alone could save Aix from her fate,
With his nostrils like pits full of blood to the brim,
And with circles of red for his eye-sockets' rim.

Then I cast loose my buffcoat, each holster let fall,
Shook off both my jack-boots, let go belt and all,
Stood up in the stirrup, leaned, patted his ear,
Called my Roland his pet-name, my horse without peer
Clapped my hands, laughed and sang, any noise, bad
    or good,
Till at length into Aix Roland galloped and stood.

And all I remember is—friends flocking round
As I sat with his head 'twixt my knees on the groun
And no voice but was praising this Roland of min
As I poured down his throat our last measure of wi
Which (the burgesses voted by common consent)
Was no more than his due who brought good ne
    from Ghent.

THEY say that news spreads like wildfire, but in advance of the telephone, radio and wireless, chances are the carrying agent was a horse. This is a poem about such a courier and not, as so many suspect, a celebration of the valiancy and the courage of the three riders. The hero of the poem is Roland. It is his performance that deserves the star billing.

Here is the Kentucky Derby of Flanders. For this poem is a horse race. The signal "They're off!" is given before the poem begins. Accordingly the pace is fast from the outset. But not even Citation can race through the work. You will have to pace yourself, varying the tempo from very fast in an abrupt change to slow. These changes should be made by stanza and follow pauses. For example, the third stanza calls for this change. The fourth for a spurt of speed. In general read the action portions at breakneck speed, the descriptive passages in the slower tempo marking. The last stanza is a happier mood, slower than the rest and more relaxed. Please remember that great speed cannot be condoned at the expense of the words and meanings; they must come out clearly. Another point to remember is that a loud voice and a fast pace are not necessarily compatible; the relationship is easily annulled.

A RED, RED ROSE
Robert Burns

O, my luve's like a red, red rose
That's newly sprung in June;
O, my luve's like the melodie
That's sweetly played in tune.

As fair thou art, my bonnie lass,
So deep in luve am I;
And I will luve thee still, my dear,
Till a' the seas gang dry.

Till a' the seas gang dry, my dear,
And the rocks melt wi' the sun;
I will luve thee still, my dear,
While the sands o' life shall run.

And fare-thee-weel, my only luve!
And fare-thee-weel a while!
And I will come again, my luve,
Though it were ten thousand m

THIS is not a poem for cynics. Don't even try to read this poem unless you are in love. This suggestion admits no future hopes and omits all past history. This is a valentine that is charged with electricity. It is vital, vibrant, allowing no insincerity and ruling out all participants who work on lend-lease. The tip-off is in the first line. His love is not like a red rose; it is like a red, red rose. It is the repetition of a conviction that admits no doubts.

The first stanza is spoken with deep feeling, but not directly to the subject. It is in the second stanza that the poet peaks directly to his love; your voice should be softer, carry breathier quality. The third stanza is pyramided squarely on op of the second; treat these two as a unit. It is from this oint that the poem builds to its climax. Remember, that the ntiment is not spoken tête à tête. The situation conveys a ggestion of a lover apart from his loved one, addressing his marks to her picture.

There are certain words that call for special emphasis: the first line the second "red." In the second "newly." In second stanza underline "deep" in the second line and 'll" in the third. In the third stanza make a note to lean "a," "melt," "still." In the last stanza take hold of "only" the first line. "Again" in the third and "were" in the last.

This is a most rewarding work. Isn't it a lovely poem!

THE WALRUS AND THE CARPENTER
Lewis Carroll

The sun was shining on the sea,
  Shining with all his might:
He did his very best to make
  The billows smooth and bright—
And this was odd, because it was
  The middle of the night.

The moon was shining sulkily,
  Because she thought the sun
Had got no business to be there
  After the day was done—
"It's very rude of him," she said,
  "To come and spoil the fun!"

The sea was wet as wet could be,
  The sands were dry as dry,
You could not see a cloud, because
  No cloud was in the sky:
No birds were flying overhead—
  There were no birds to fly.

The Walrus and the Carpenter
    Were walking close at hand:
They wept like anything to see
    Such quantities of sand:
"If this were only cleared away,"
    They said, "it would be grand!"

"If seven maids with seven mops
    Swept it for half a year,
Do you suppose," the Walrus said,
    "That they could get it clear?"
"I doubt it," said the Carpenter,
    And shed a bitter tear.

"O Oysters, come and walk with us!"
    The Walrus did beseech.
"A pleasant walk, a pleasant talk,
    Along the briny beach:
We cannot do with more than four,
    To give a hand to each."

The eldest Oyster looked at him,
    But never a word he said:
The eldest Oyster winked his eye,
    And shook his heavy head—
Meaning to say he did not choose
    To leave the oyster-bed.

But four young Oysters hurried up,
    All eager for the treat:
Their coats were brushed, their faces washed,
    Their shoes were clean and neat—
And this was odd, because, you know,
    They hadn't any feet.

Four other Oysters followed them,
    And yet another four;
And thick and fast they came at last,
    And more, and more, and more—
All hopping through the frothy waves,
    And scrambling to the shore.

The Walrus and the Carpenter
    Walked on a mile or so,
And then they rested on a rock
    Conveniently low:
And all the little Oysters stood
    And waited in a row.

"The time has come," the Walrus said,
    "To talk of many things:
Of shoes—and ships—and sealing wax—
    Of cabbages—and kings—
And why the sea is boiling hot—
    And whether pigs have wings."

"But wait a bit," the Oysters cried,
    "Before we have our chat;
For some of us are out of breath,
    And all of us are fat!"
"No hurry!" said the Carpenter,
    They thanked him much for that.

"A loaf of bread," the Walrus said,
    "Is what we chiefly need:
Pepper and vinegar besides
    Are very good indeed—
Now, if you're ready, Oysters dear,
    We can begin to feed."

"But not on us!" the Oysters cried,
    Turning a little blue.
"After such kindness, that would be
    A dismal thing to do!"
"The night is fine," the Walrus said,
    "Do you admire the view?

"It was so kind of you to come!
    And you are very nice!"
The Carpenter said nothing but
    "Cut us another slice.
I wish you were not quite so deaf—
    I've had to ask you twice!"

"It seems a shame," the Walrus said,
  "To play them such a trick.
After we've brought them out so far,
  And made them trot so quick!"
The Carpenter said nothing but
  "The butter's spread too thick!"

"I weep for you," the Walrus said:
  "I deeply sympathize."
With sobs and tears he sorted out
  Those of the largest size,
Holding his pocket-handkerchief
  Before his streaming eyes.

"O Oysters," said the Carpenter,
  "You've had a pleasant run!
Shall we be trotting home again?"
  But answer came there none—
And this was scarcely odd, because
  They'd eaten every one.

Readings of "The Walrus and the Carpenter" always R in season. A classic that appeals both to the esthetes and the athletes of the mind. It has been the object of careful scrutiny— a diligent searching for a moral or a point. But there is no point here; not even a bluepoint. (A pun permitted by Dr. Dodgson's own example which we have followed by intent rather than content.) This is sheer nonsense, deriving its qualities from the picture making ability of the author. It is almost an abstract painting. If you try to take this poem seriously, you will realize that this is a poem of gangsterism; the Walrus and the Carpenter act like two hoods from a Chicago mob. But don't try to look at this piece through your previous spectacles. It's for fun. These are wonderful images: the Walrus and the Carpenter walking hand in hand (probably looking very much alike), the fat little oysters running along the beach. Doesn't it remind you of a Walt Disney production?

The actual reading calls for a rather brisk pace, spiced by a series of *sotto voce* asides. Take the first stanza. The first four lines paint a picture; the last two debunk it. This happens again and again: look at the double aside in the third stanza, again at the seventh. Nonsense, like Farce, must be played straight. One cannot read a piece like this and editorialize by reacting to it within the body of the performance. The reaction is strictly the privilege of the listener.

Aim your readings for the bull's-eye of chuckles, rather than for laughs. This is a smiling poem. The annotator would like to suggest that attempts to characterize the dramatis personae will spoil the poem. Although there are many temptations to make noises like a walrus, a carpenter, or an oyster, these will be in effect acts of isolation that will make your reading

However, while you will not want to change your tonal cteristics, you can achieve the needed effect by using a rent rhythm as each character speaks. Try a syncopated ding of these lines in the exact meter of the lines.

Before you open the throttle of your reading, measure this poem carefully. There are many interesting nuances that you will want to note before proceeding at full speed. For example: the sun is masculine, the moon is feminine. The adjectives and adverbs are important touches (the moon was shining sulkily). Lean slightly on these little flairs without overaccenting them. Keep a straight face throughout.

OUR LITTLE LIFE
William Shakespeare

Our revels now are ended. These, our actors,
As I foretold you, were all spirits, and
Are melted into air, into thin air:
And, like the baseless fabric of this vision,
The cloud-capp'd towers, the gorgeous palaces,
The solemn temples, the great globe itself,
Yea, all which it inherit, shall dissolve;
And, like this insubstantial pageant faded,
Leave not a rack behind. We are such stuff
As dreams are made on, and our little life
Is rounded with a sleep.

(*from* THE TEMPEST)

A S the closing poem of this volume, this excerpt from Shakespeare's *The Tempest* is the turning-down of the lights. Arnold Moss, who read this work for our Decca recorded treasury, recalled one of the touching moments of the present-day American Theatre. It was the night that the wartime President Franklin D. Roosevelt died. Set against that contemporary tragedy, the lines of this piece moved both actor and audience to tears. It is a positive demonstration of our concept of setting classic pieces in contemporary frames.

The excerpt itself is both envoi and warning. It suggests that reality is something that must be faced; that people are not like actors playing their part and then disappearing behind the falling curtain. In life this is not possible; last night's grand excitement is followed relentlessly by today's realities. Yet, in returning to our apartment house after spending some time in our castle in the air, there is an understandable reluctance. We hesitate to give up the easy way. This keynotes the tempo of the reading. It is slow, but not dragging. Reluctant is the best word. Your interpretive clock should read, "the moment before the curtain falls." You are straddling today and tomorrow.

Emphasize "revels" in the first line, "melted" and "thin" in the third, "baseless" in the fourth, "cloud-capped," "gorgeous" in the fifth, "solemn" and "great" in the sixth. In the seventh "all." In the eighth, "insubstantial." "Leave" in the ninth as well as "We." Second line from the end "little." Underline these words. Emphasis, in the tempo suggested in this reading, can be effectively portrayed not by increasing volume but by holding these words slightly, with a moment pause before moving along.

This is an anthology of the Spoken Word and we have added a few punctuation marks to some of the standard text to help you mould your interpretation.

Our revels now are ended.

CATALOGUE OF DRAMATIC RECORDINGS

FORGERY is a crime both in the statute books of law and the "prompt" books of the theatre. Imitation may be the sincerest form of flattery, but interpretive imitation belongs in the tool chest of the mimics rather than in the talent inventory of a creative performer. Imitation dilutes or cancels out the instincts of performance.

Despite the danger of copying, we append a list of available dramatic recordings. The artists whose abilities are sealed in the wax of these recorded items can give valuable lessons in technique. But no self-respecting musical conductor engaged to lead a Philharmonic in a performance of Beethoven's Fifth copies the tempo, shadings and conception of Toscanini's recording, even though as a musical experience it is both inevitable and important. So, we append this important list with the fervent hope that the reader will use it as an observatory rather than a stencil.

Soon, it is hoped, the interpretations of the three artists (Raymond Edward Johnson, Jay Jostyn and Arnold Moss) whose work on the original transcriptions sparked this volume into being will shortly be available on radio stations throughout the United States and Canada, as well as on Decca Records. For your reference, here is a check list of material that is generally available in a well-stocked record store.

OUR AMERICAN HERITAGE

Here are great poems celebrating milestones in the History of America, including:

THE STAR-SPANGLED BANNER . . . . . . Key
OLD IRONSIDES . . . . Holmes
HAIL, COLUMBIA . . . . Hopkinson
WARREN'S ADDRESS TO AMERICAN SOLDIERS . Pierpont
CONCORD HYMN . . . . Emerson
LINCOLN, THE MAN OF THE PEOPLE . . Markham
NANCY HANKS . . . . Benet
LANDING OF THE PILGRIM FATHERS . . . Hemans
BARBARA FRIETCHIE . . . . Whittier
COLUMBUS . . . . Miller
THE AMERICAN FLAG . . . . Drake
PAUL REVERE'S RIDE . . . . Longfellow
AMERICA . . . . Smith
SHERIDAN'S RIDE . . . . Read

The readers include Pat O'Brien, Bing Crosby, Walter Huston, Agnes Moorehead, Frederic March and Brian Donlevy. Of particular interest is Bing Crosby's recitation of the National Anthem. This is one of the most exciting albums of dramatic readings ever made available to the public.

Decca, No. A-53

THE CRISIS

Paul Muni gives a restrained reading of Thomas Paine's American classic.

Victor, No. 10-1005

LINCOLN'S GETTYSBURG ADDRESS

Two versions of this immortal speech are currently available; both are discussed in this volume. The Charles Laughton piece is on *Columbia Records, No. S-271M*. The Massey version is on *Linguaphone, listed by title only*.

A third version by Orson Welles is in *Decca Album, A-439*.

Another reading by Melvyn Douglas is in *Victor Album, DM 1088*.

ON A NOTE OF TRIUMPH

Norman Corwin wrote a brilliant celebration of victory in the war, and it was broadcast with a narration by Martin Gabel that was of matching brilliance. This is a worthy and lasting recording of America's victory, commemorating that broadcast.

Columbia, No. M-575

NO MAN IS AN ISLAND

Presented here is a collection of speeches on the interdependence of men with excerpts from the pens of Pericles, Paine, Patrick Henry, Daniel Webster, John Brown, Emile Zola and Abraham Lincoln. Orson Welles at his thrilling best is the reader. It is regrettable that many of these dramatic albums are recorded on shellac biscuits rather than on surface noise-free vinylite: after a few playings the scratch noise and the artist's voice fight for the dominant position.

Decca, A-439

THE PEOPLE, YES

Carl Sandburg reads his own masterful work. He makes no pretentions to stardom but mixes sincerity with his calico touch. Here is poetry wearing blue jeans.

Decca, DA-273

MINE EYES HAVE SEEN THE GLORY

This is a fervid group of readings by one of America's most distinguished actresses, Helen Hayes. Included are:

PLEDGE TO THE FLAG
BEAT! BEAT! DRUMS . . . . Whitman
STAR-SPANGLED BANNER . . . . Key
AMERICA . . . . Smith
BATTLE HYMN OF THE REPUBLIC . . . . . Howe

As an interesting comparison based on our annotation of "The Star-Spangled Banner," compare this reading of the National Anthem by Miss Hayes with Bing Crosby's on *Decca, A-536*. Here is the perfect sample of the way it is possible to reach two end products with the same material. Both have their merits.

Victor, M-909

AMERICA WAS PROMISES

Archibald MacLeish, ex-Congressional Librarian and generally American poet laureate, recreates his American epic "America Was Promises." A sincere reading is the result.

Linguaphone, L

IN THE AMERICAN TRADITION

Orson Welles here elects himself president four times and is entitled to a vote of confidence. Mr. Welles has a "White House" voice.

JEFFERSON—FIRST INAUGURAL ADDRESS
LINCOLN—SECOND INAUGURAL ADDRESS
WILSON—ADDRESS TO THE PEACE CONFERENCE
ROOSEVELT, F. D.—FIRST WAR ADDRESS

Decca, 394

ABE LINCOLN IN ILLINOIS

Here is a recording of Robert E. Sherwood's Pulitzer Prize play with the famous and definitive reading of the Lincoln role by Raymond Massey. His many appearances as Lincoln have made all other portrayals stand up for comparison. It has been said of Mr. Massey that he has played Lincoln so often he will probably have to be assassinated. Note, particularly, his restrained yet easy delivery. It sounds easy but remains hard to duplicate.

Victor, M-591

JUDITH ANDERSON IN DRAMATIC SKETCHES

The American Theatre, famed for the number of its "First Ladies," must put Judith Anderson near the head of the list. Miss Anderson marries a superb voice to a superb technique demonstrating the reward of dramatic control. This album contains:

THE STATUE OF LIBERTY . . . . . . Latouche
LETTER TO MRS. BIXBY . . . . Lincoln
THE FOG . . . . Latouche
THE SERMON ON THE MOUNT

Victor, DM-960

THE SHAKESPEARE MEMORIAL THEATRE SERIES

The home team is at bat in this album series. The Shakespeare Memorial Theatre Series, recorded by members of the Stratford-Upon-Avon Festival Company, has produced four albums. Three are listed below. The fourth, Othello, is in the process of preparation. These performances are honest, simple, and forthright. They lack the virtuosity of some of the other available Shakespearean productions. Valuable both as a yardstick and as source material, many of the speeches recorded in these albums are unavailable elsewhere.

THE MERRY WIVES OF WINDSOR BA-1
THE TEMPEST BA-2
RICHARD II BA-3

Britam Agencies

SCENES FROM SHAKESPEARE'S PLAYS

Otis Skinner and Cornelia Otis Skinner have recorded excerpts from six Shakespearean works:

MACBETH
TAMING OF THE SHREW
JULIUS CAESAR
ROMEO AND JULIET
MERCHANT OF VENICE
AS YOU LIKE IT

Victor, M-753

JOHN GIELGUD IN SHAKESPEAREAN WORKS

Mr. Gielgud's interpretations of Shakespeare must command the attention of every student. These works were recorded in London, and released in this country under the aegis of the Linguaphone Institute.

MERCHANT OF VENICE—Act I, Scene 1
Gratiano's Speech

As You Like It—Act II, Scene 7
    "A fool, a fool . . ."
King Richard II—Act II, Scene 1
    John of Gaunt's Speech
Sonnet 106
As You Like It—Act II, Scene 7
    Jacques' Speech
The Tempest—Act IV, Scene 1
    Prospero's Speech
King Henry V—Act III, Scene 1
    King Henry's Speech
King Henry IV—Act I, Scene 3
    Hotspur's Speech
Othello—Act I, Scene 3
    Othello's Speech
Hamlet—Act II, Scene 2
    Hamlet's Speech
Hamlet—Act IV, Scene 4
    Hamlet's Speech
Sonnet 18
King Richard II—Act III, Scene 3
    King Richard's Speech
King Henry V—Act IV, Scene 3
    King Henry's Speech
A Midsummer Night's Dream—Act II, Scene 1
    Oberon's Speech
             Linguaphone, EEG-30E, 32E, 33E, 34E

JOHN BARRYMORE

Fabled and fabulous, the Great Profile demonstrates his Shakespearean talents recorded near to and sometimes at the height of his powers.

    Hamlet's Soliloquy (Now I am Alone)
    Gloucester's Soliloquy (Ay, Edward Will
      Use Women)   *Victor, 6827*

THE MERCURY THEATRE

These albums by Orson Welles and his supporting players of the Mercury Theatre demonstrate the ability of this group which punched tradition in the nose and made Broadway exciting for several years. These are heavy and expensive albums, but worth the price and the time.

JULIUS CAESAR

Columbia, C-10

MACBETH

Columbia, C-33

MERCHANT OF VENICE

Columbia, C-66

MACBETH

This is an interpretation of sheer virtuosity masterfully blended by Maurice Evans and Judith Anderson. The powerful scenes are portrayed with vitality and depth.

Victor, M-878

HAMLET

Just released as this volume was going to press, this had to be included. It is magnificent dramatic verse and magnificent dramatic acting combined superbly. Laurence Olivier is The Melancholy Dane, and "out of this world" is our opinion of his performance.

Victor, DM-1273

HAMLET

Mr. Evans plays Hamlet as though there were a psycho analyst waiting in the wings. One gets a sense of over-orches tration, though Mr. Evans' voice is brilliant music. Check thi reading against the Laurence Olivier version and the Joh Barrymore performance.

Columbia, M-3

OTHELLO

Paul Robeson, of the mighty voice, plays the jealous Moor with the members of the original Broadway company. Mr. Robeson's voice is like a shaft of steel, and is surely more pliable in song than in speech. Jose Ferrer's Iago is a masterpiece and a continuing dramatic lesson to all members of both the inner circle and the periphery of the theatre trade. This project (for it is in three albums) is worth having and studying.

Columbia, MM-554

ROMEO AND JULIET

The Ham and Eggs of dramatic records, Gielgud and Shakespeare, team up again. Records were not available for review at press time. Also in ANTA series, Mr. Gielgud has performed John of Gaunt's speeches from Richard the Second. This is to be released as a single record. Fortunately this material is being pressed on unbreakable vinylite with a resulting minimum of scratch noise.

Decca, (unnumbered at press time)

RICHARD THE SECOND

Maurice Evans highlights scenes from this play with a definitive performance on records. Mr. Evans' technique of holding on to his vowels is interesting to observe.

Columbia, MM-303

HENRY V

Laurence Olivier is one of the two greatest living actors. (The modification is in the name of safety.) Listen to the superb technique of this master artist in scenes taken from sound track of the award-winning film.

Victor, DM-1128

MEDEA

Suffering, which reaches a daily low on radio's Soap Operas, is given a classical touch by the brilliance of Judith Anderson. A virtuoso performance full of pyrotechnics. This is the hardest kind of performance to give, but Miss Anderson fills the playbill—to perfection.

Decca, DAU-12

THE MASTERPIECES OF LITERATURE—VOLUME I

Radio's poet laureate, Norman Corwin, reads the works of other poet laureates. Interesting and simple readings, they are more valuable for their conception than for the reader's technique.

BOOTS	Kipling
SEA FEVER	Masefield
BOOT AND SADDLE	Browning
A RED, RED ROSE	Burns
BREAK, BREAK, BREAK	Tennyson
KUBLA KHAN	Coleridge
THE LARK	Reese
SONG OF THE CHATTAHOOCHEE	Lanier
FROM THE SANTA FE TRAIL	Lindsay
LOST	Sandburg
SILVER	de la Mare
THE RUNAWAY	Frost
A WET SHEET AND A FLOWING SEA	Cunningham
THE FOG	Sandburg
THE RAILWAY TRAIN	Dickinson
DESERTED	Cawein
IN TIME OF "THE BREAKING OF NATIONS"	Hardy
CROSSING THE BAR	Tennyson
OZYMANDIAS	Shelley
THE TIGER	Blake
SHE WALKS IN BEAUTY	Byron

DOVER BEACH . . . . Arnold
ENCOURAGEMENT TO A LOVER . . . . . Suckling
ON HIS BLINDNESS . . . . Milton
IN FLANDERS FIELD . . . . McCrae
WHEN I HEARD THE LEARN'D ASTRONOMER . Whitman
TO ALTHEA, FROM PRISON . . . . . . Lovelace
NOVEMBER NIGHT . . . . Crapsey
THE MAN WITH THE HOE . . . . . . Markham

Columbia, E-5

THE MASTERPIECES OF LITERATURE—VOLUME II

Wesley Addy presents a recorded parallel to the current Freedom Train exhibit.

THE MAYFLOWER COMPACT
    From the Pennsylvania Charter of Privileges
    (October 28, 1701)
DECLARATION OF INDEPENDENCE . . Thomas Jefferson
SELECTIONS FROM THE FAREWELL ADDRESS OF
    GEORGE WASHINGTON
FROM THE FIRST INAUGURAL ADDRESS OF
    THOMAS JEFFERSON
A SELECTION FROM SACRED OBLIGATIONS
    Daniel Webster
THE GETTYSBURG ADDRESS . . . Abraham Lincoln
FROM THE HISTORY OF LIBERTY . . Edward Everett
PATRIOTISM . . . . Lyman Abbott
FROM A PAN-AMERICAN POLICY . . . . Elihu Root
FROM OUR RESPONSIBILITIES AS A NATION
    Theodore Roosevelt
FROM AMERICANS OF FOREIGN BIRTH
    Woodrow Wilson
FROM THE PROMISED LAND . . . . . Mary Antin

Columbia, E-6

THE MASTERPIECES OF LITERATURE—VOLUME III

(Poetry, Volume II)

Basil Rathbone recites in all his British resonance. He is a solid artist who stands on the platform of simplicity. Regrettably, he uses an announcement of what he is about to read, a device which we find a disturbing preamble. However, this album is designed for school use and this announcement may therefore be justified on educational grounds. Mr. Rathbone's readings are sometimes too rapid for our taste, but his pyrotechnics are not frightening. This album could be a valuable companion to this volume. Included are:

ABOU BEN ADHEM . . . . Hunt
AMERICA . . . . Lanier
ARROW AND THE SONG . . . . Longfellow
GO, LOVELY ROSE . . . . Waller
GOD'S WORLD . . . . Millay
HATE . . . . Stephens
IN MEMORIAM . . . . Tennyson
IN MEMORIAM . . . . Stevenson
INVICTUS . . . . Henle
LOVELIEST OF TREES . . . . Housma
MY OWN, MY NATIVE LAND . . . . . . Sco
ODE TO THE WEST WIND . . . . . . Shell
ODE TO A GRECIAN URN . . . . Kea
OLD WOMAN OF THE ROADS . . . . . Colu
ON FIRST LOOKING INTO CHAPMAN'S HOMER . Ke
ON THE LATE MASSACRE IN PIEDMONT . . Milt
PASSIONATE SHEPHERD TO HIS LOVE, THE . Marlo
PROSPICE . . . . Brown
SAY NOT THE STRUGGLE . . . . Clo
SONNET . . . . Bro
SONNET XLIII . . . . E. B. Brown
SONNET XXIX . . . . Shakesp
STUPIDITY STREET . . . . Hod

To a Waterfowl . . . . Bryant
To the Virgins, to Make Much of Time . Herrick
Travel . . . . Millay
Vagabond, The . . . . Stevenson
Waste Places, The . . . . Stephens
World is Too Much With Us, The . Wordsworth

Columbia, E-11

THE VOICE OF POETRY—VOLUME I

Edith Evans, a gifted reader of the English school, presents a group of well-known poems.

To Me Fair Friend . . . . Shakespeare
To Celia . . . . Jonson
A Slumber Did My Spirit Seal . . . Wordsworth
La Belle Dame Sans Merci . . . . . Keats
The Tiger . . . . Blake
Say Not the Struggle Naught Availeth . Clough
She Walks in Beauty . . . . Byron
Upon Westminster Bridge . . . . Wordsworth
Allan-a-Dale . . . . Scott
Sonnet CXVI—Let Me Not to the Marriage
    of True Minds
Sonnet XXX—When to the Sessions of
    Sweet Silent Thought
"Cymbeline"—Fear No More the Heat
    O' the Sun . . . . Shakespeare
The Reaper . . . . Wordsworth
Sweet and Low . . . . Tennyson
A Child's Grace . . . . Herrick
Nicholas Nye . . . . de la Mare
The Shyness of Beauty . . . . . . Binyon
Tewkesbury Road . . . . Masefield
The Donkey . . . . Chesterton
Weathers . . . . Hardy

CARGOES . . . . Masefield
THE PLOUGHMAN . . . . Bottomley
SUMMER MORNING . . . . Nichols
THE KINGFISHERS . . . . Davies
THE SONG OF ENCHANTMENT . . . . de la Mare
YOU ARE OLD, FATHER WILLIAM . . . . Carroll
THE ROLLING ENGLISH ROAD . . . . Chesterton
THE GIRL . . . . Church
THE ELFIN ARTIST . . . . Noyes
THE MOON . . . . Davies

Columbia, M-375

THE VOICE OF POETRY—VOLUME II

The reader of this volume is John Gielgud. His name is a trademark that guarantees an incisive and brittle interpretation.

GO LOVELY ROSE . . . . Waller
SINCE FIRST I SAW YOUR FACE . . . Anon. ca 1607
THE TRIUMPH . . . . Jonson
THAT TIME OF YEAR . . . . Shakespeare
ODE TO THE WEST WIND . . . . . . Shelley
OZYMANDIAS . . . . Shelley
DEATH . . . . Donne
SO WE'LL GO NO MORE A-ROVING . . . Byron
YOUNG AND OLD . . . . Kingsley
A BIRTHDAY . . . . Rossetti
SUMMER DAWN . . . . Morris
BREAK, BREAK, BREAK . . . . Tennyson
THE STORM IS OVER . . . . Bridges
LONE HEART, LEARNING . . . . . . Sassoon
DOWN THE GLIMMERING STAIRCASE . . . Sassoon
ARABIA . . . . de la Mare
TRUTH . . . . Masefield

LEISURE . . . . Davies
SILVER . . . . de la Mare
THE JOURNEY OF THE MAGI . . . . Eliot
PRELUDES . . . . Eliot

Columbia, M-419

THE SONG OF SONGS

King Solomon is interpreted by the King of Readers. Perhaps this is the best of the Orson Welles records. Sheer beauty, this reading.

Decca, 29157

RUBAIYAT OF OMAR KHAYYAM

An abridgement of the famed masterpiece is read with proper musical backgrounds by stage and screen actor Ralph Bellamy.

Victor, DM-1055

OSCAR WILDE

Scenes from two plays of Oscar Wilde are acted by John Gielgud and company (on an unbreakable record). Mr. Gielgud is superb in these comedy gems; his timing is razor sharp.

THE IMPORTANCE OF BEING EARNEST—ACT I
LADY WINDEMERE'S FAN—ACT III

Decca, DU-90012

THE PIED PIPER OF HAMELIN

Robert Browning's classic provides a field day for actress Ingrid Bergman; Miss Bergman does all the parts. Both as an exercise in virtuosity and a neat re-creation of an old warhorse, Miss Bergman demonstrates that reading like painting has a white canvas on which the interpreter can paint in many colors. Here is a demonstration of the existence of a vocal pallette that must be used to shade and highlight any reading.

Decca, DA-450

THE CHILDREN'S HOUR

Longfellow poems are given simple readings by movie actor Donald Crisp. Since so many of Longfellow's works are incorporated in this Treasury, check this professional's work against your own results. Performance is nice—but perhaps a shade too crisp.

THE CHILDREN'S HOUR
THE RAINY DAY
HYMN TO THE NIGHT
A PSALM OF LIFE
THE ARROW AND THE SONG
THE VILLAGE BLACKSMITH
THE DAY IS DONE
THE BUILDING OF THE SHIP

Decca, A-434

LEAVES OF GRASS

Mr. Bellamy recites again, this time giving highlights from Walt Whitman's book of greatness. Whitman is one of the hardest poets to read aloud. It is interesting to check Mr. Bellamy's reading against your own ideas. Included are:

TO A CERTAIN CIVILIAN
I THINK I COULD TURN AND LIVE WITH ANIMALS
TO THE MAN OF WAR BIRD
FOR YOU O DEMOCRACY
VIGIL STRANGE I KEPT ON THE FIELD ONE NIGHT
LONG, TOO LONG AMERICA
OVER THE CARNAGE ROSE PROPHETIC A VOICE

O STAR OF FRANCE
TO A FOIL'D EUROPEAN REVOLUTIONAIRE
EUROPE
FRANCE
A BROADWAY PAGEANT
YEARS OF THE MODERN
I WAS LOOKING A LONG WHILE
PASSAGE TO INDIA
BY BLUE ONTARIO'S SHORE
SO LONG! .
SONG OF THE OPEN ROAD

Victor, M-955

THE MAN WITH THE HOE

Edwin Markham in the later stages of his life reads his masterpiece. Not a professional reader, Mr. Markham makes this record a sentimental souvenir rather than a guidepost to the student.

Timely, 1000-A

ETHAN FROME

Star billing is shared by Raymond Massey and Ruth Gordon. Able performers, they display a consistency of values that has distinguished their every appearance whether on screen, stage, radio or disc. Listen to this album for its interplay.

Decca, (unnumbered at press time)

POEMS BY EDNA ST. VINCENT MILLAY

Poets are sometimes more at home with their pens than their voices. Yet their readings are important clues to interpretation. Too often the creator tries to run the relay race by himself instead of passing the baton on to the interpreter.

Here, Basil Rathbone is the interpreter and he makes a genuine contribution to the development of the author's work.

THE BALLAD OF THE HARP-WEAVER
SONNETS FROM "FATAL INTERVIEW"
THIS BEAST THAT RENDS ME, No. 2
NOT IN A SILVER CASKET, No. 11
LOVE IS NOT ALL, No. 30
SORROWFUL DREAMS, No. 33
OH, SLEEP FOREVER, No. 52
ELEGY
CHILDHOOD IS THE KINGDOM
RECUERDO
I SHALL FORGET YOU PRESENTLY, MY DEAR
RETURN FROM TOWN
PORTRAIT BY A NEIGHBOR
TRAVEL
TO PAO-CHIN
THE ANGUISH
I MUST NOT DIE OF PITY
THE MAID OF ORLEANS
WHERE CAN THE HEART BE HIDDEN
RENASCENCE

Columbia Masterworks Series, By Title

E. E. CUMMINGS

Another author speaks his piece. Mr. Cummings reads

POEM OR BEAUTY HURTS MR. VINAL
ITEM
BUFFALO BILL
SOMEWHERE I HAVE TRAVELLED
IN JUST SPRING
SEVEN POEMS
OH, SWEET SPONTANEOUS EARTH
SINCE FEELING IS FIRST

Linguaphone, By T

THE HARVARD VOCARIUM

Harvard University has established a unique and excellent service to those interested in poetry. In this, the first library of its kind, there may be found authors reading their own works, a valuable experience for those who are interested in these artists' interpretation of their own creations.

Poets whose records may be purchased are:

RIGLEY TORRENCE

TENNESSEE WILLIAMS
ROBERT PENN WARREN
RIDGLEY TORRENCE
CHRISTOPHER LA FARGE
ROBINSON JEFFERS
T. S. ELIOT
W. H. AUDEN

Among the dramatic records available are:

Flora Robson in the Sleepwalking Scene from MACBETH
Walter Hampden and Bobby Clark in Sheridan's
THE RIVALS

The Harvard Vocarium address: Harvard College Library, Cambridge 38, Massachusetts.

SPOKEN ENGLISH AND BROKEN ENGLISH

Never willing to be outdone by the Bard, Mr. George Bernard Shaw has provided his own kind of "Advice to the Players." This four-sided work is amusing and instructive and spoken by Mr. Shaw in person.

Linguaphone, L-3

VICTORIA REGINA

This is a recorded translation of one of Helen Hayes' most brilliant successes. Miss Hayes has all the skill and in-tenseness of a surgeon; her diction is sharp and brilliant. This album is one of a series currently being recorded and released by the imaginative Decca crew. It is part of an overall project undertaken by Decca and the American National Theatre Academy. The leading artists who star in these albums perform as a public service with royalties accruing to ANTA. Simon Rady is the series director.

Decca, (unnumbered at press time)

THE SKIN OF OUR TEETH

Thornton Wilder's Pulitzer Prize winner in an album featuring three highlight scenes. Miss Bankhead re-establishes her definitive performance. Her distinctive vocal style may only be described as a cross between "sandpaper" and "velvet." It is interesting to note how a stylized performer such as Miss Bankhead integrates her style in ensemble work and comes out completely believable.

Decca, (unnumbered at press time)

DOROTHY PARKER POEMS AND PROSE

Ilka Chase who reads this album, and Dorothy Parke who wrote it, are tweedle dee and tweedle dum. Miss Park has acid in her pen and Miss Chase, the same in her voic It's a brilliant collaboration. The student will be especia interested in Miss Chase's timing—it is superb.

THE MAIL-SERVANT AT THE INN
INVENTORY
THE SECOND OLDEST STORY
DAY DREAMS
THE BURNED CHILD
THE LITTLE OLD LADY IN LAVENDER SILK

NEWS ITEMS
CHANT FOR DARK HOURS
SURPRISE
RESUME
THE THIN EDGE
TOMBSTONES IN THE STARLIGHT
TWO-VOLUME NOVEL
AFTERNOON
PARABLE FOR A CERTAIN VIRGIN
SENTIMENT

Victor, MO-971

THE FACE IS FAMILIAR

Ogden Nash has edited a vocal anthology of his own poems with a Bing Crosby-ish touch. Here in an unprofessional voice infringing on his own copyrights in a manner casual and reminiscent of a father saying, "Oh, I just happen to have a few pictures of my children in my wallet." Mr. Nash, as a reader, is pleasant and nasal, but authentic.

TWO AND ONE ARE A PROBLEM
THE INDIVIDUALIST
I HAVE IT ON GOOD AUTHORITY
BANKERS ARE JUST LIKE ANYBODY ELSE
    EXCEPT RICHER
THE COMMON COLD
ISN'T NATURE WONDERFUL
SEASIDE SERENADE
THE DROP OF A HAT
ONE THIRD OF A CALENDAR
TRAVELER'S REST
THE HUSBAND'S LAMENT

Decca, 342

✓

SORRY, WRONG NUMBER

Here is an inspired and inspirational achievement by Agnes Moorehead in a role she created on the radio. Pay particular attention to the dynamics of intensity she creates and her brilliant use of change of pace.

Decca, DAU-2

TALES FROM THE OLD COUNTRY

Sholem Aleichem's stories have been albumized by Howard DaSilva. This is a worthy album both for entertainment and study. We hear in these three stories a perfect example of "character-narration"; the narrator effectively creates the folk mood inherent in the writing. He *is* and he *tells* simultaneously. It's a difficult task and a superb result.

Decca, DU-5

I CAN HEAR IT NOW

Here is what the history books of tomorrow should be Edward R. Murrow, who combines new sense with an exciting narrative style, has recreated history by piecing together slice of the actual voices and sounds of some of the most dramati years of mankind. The oratorical mastery of Churchill an Roosevelt, the voice of an abdicating English King, the w of the American humorist, Will Rogers, the intensity of a American baseball player, Lou Gehrig, are some of the elemen in this album. Sports announcers and world leaders all ha vital lessons to offer to the would-be performer. Reality alwa holds the first mortgage on any art. Jack Gude was the produ and Fred W. Friendly collaborated behind the scenes with M Murrow. Available both in standard-sized, twelve-inch albu and in the new, long-playing record technique.

Columbia, MM-

INDEX

INDEX OF TITLES AND AUTHORS

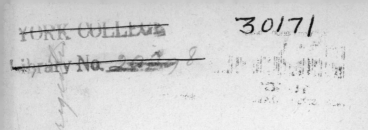